For Peg

[handwritten inscription, largely illegible cursive]

Sept 9, 2000

IN THE FOOTSTEPS
OF THE GODDESS

ALSO BY CRISTINA BIAGGI

Habitations of the Great Goddess

IN THE
FOOTSTEPS
OF THE
GODDESS

Personal Stories

EDITED & ILLUSTRATED BY
CRISTINA BIAGGI, Ph.D.

FOREWORD BY STARHAWK

KNOWLEDGE, IDEAS & TRENDS, INC.
MANCHESTER, CT

Cover art and interior illustrations: Cristina Biaggi
Cover design: Sonja Hakala and Wendy MacMillen
Text design and production: Sonja Hakala
Managing editor: Sonja Hakala

First published in 2000 by Knowledge, Ideas & Trends, Inc.
KIT: The Positive Publisher
1131-0 Tolland Turnpike, Suite 175
Manchester, CT 06040
(800) 826-0529
www.booktrends.com
Knowledge, Ideas & Trends, Inc. books are available for bulk purchase and customization purchases by corporations and other organizations for promotion and premiums. Contact the special sales department at the above address.

Library of Congress Cataloging-in-Publication Data

In the footsteps of the goddess : personal stories / edited and illustrated by Cristina Biaggi.-- 1st ed.
     p. cm.
   Includes biographical references.
   ISBN 1-879198-30-4 (pbk. : alk.paper)
     1. Goddess religion. 2. Feminist spirituality. 3. Spiritual biography.
     I. Biaggi, Cristina
   BL473.5.I5 2000
   291.2'114--dc21

First edition
10 9 8 7 6 5 4 3 2 1

To my dear partner Pattie

Contents

Foreword

$\mathcal{M}$any years ago, I was asked by priest and author Matthew Fox to teach a course in Feminist Theology at the Institute which he had founded. I promptly renamed the course "Feminist Thealogy," the change in spelling reflecting a shift in focus from *Theos,* God, to *Thea,* Goddess. Beyond that point I wasn't sure where to begin. By that time in my life, I had been a priestess of the Goddess for many years. I had written books about feminist spirituality and taught many, many people how to create ritual and how to put the Earth at the center of their spiritual life. But I had no formal training in theology—or thealogy either. Although I had a strong educational background in the Jewish teachings of my ancestors, my university studies had focused on art, film, and psychology, not religion.

How might a feminist approach thealogy? I wondered. The question brought me back to my first experiences in the feminist revival of the early seventies. I was a student in my twenties, eagerly reading Kate Millett and Gloria Steinem, devouring the first issues of *Ms.* magazine, and meeting with my consciousness-raising group. Each week, we would gather, choose a topic and then speak to it from our own experience. As women, we felt trapped in a world defined by men, and interpreted by male theories not designed to reflect the truth of women. How could we take action, how could we make choices about ideology or strategy, when all our theories were constructed by our oppressors? As Audre Lorde expressed it, "The master's tools will never dismantle the master's house."

It seemed the only tool we had, the only untainted source of knowledge, was our own experience as women. And so women began talking to each other, in small groups, practicing the discipline of listening to each other without interrupting, speaking honestly about the basic issues of our lives: our bodies, our mothers, our sexuality, our children, our work. Out of those conversations arose the feminist agenda of the last thirty years.

I decided to model my Feminist Thealogy class on a consciousness-raising group. We began by going around the room, giving each person a chance to speak about her or his real experience of Goddess/God. The conversation was emotional and deeply moving. We heard tales of unexpected joy and of finding the sacred in moments of deepest grief, stories of wonder, and of the strength that comes from despair. The class included not just Goddess worshippers but priests, nuns, ministers, and religious teachers. I was amazed to learn that many of them, in all their years of formal religious instruction, had never been asked how they actually experienced their God. In teaching the class again and again, hearing story after story, I was struck by the themes that emerged and how identical they were to the traditional associations of the Goddess with birth, death, growth, healing, nature, and regeneration.

A feminist thealogy, I began to believe, would not be a list of attributes of the deity or dogmas one must accept. A feminist thealogy would be descriptive rather than prescriptive: a collection of travelers' tales, a set of road maps, a list of sightings. Now Cristina Biaggi has given us that thealogy. In asking hundreds of women and men to describe their actual experience of the Goddess, she has brought us into a vast collective consciousness-raising group.

The stories in this book are full of wonder and diversity. Linda Johnsen experiences limitless, ecstatic consciousness when walking across the dining room as a young teenager. Beth Hensperger nearly loses her life in a snowstorm, but is sent back to life by the woman under the sea.

Miriam Robbins Dexter sees the Goddess in living waters, Karen London and Monica Sjöö find Her in giving birth. Ubaka Hill finds in Her the missing, nurturing mother she needs in her own life. For Glenda Cloughley, She is the round contours of the New Zealand landscape. Vicki Noble reaches the visceral understanding that "Her body is my body."

At times, the Goddess appears in concrete form: a live peacock appears to Barbara Harrell in a moment of spiritual crisis, a hawk swoops down on Lucy Harrison when she calls on Inanna during a funeral. Diana Marto encounters a bobcat. Some women literally hear the Goddess as a voice. She appears to Patricia Healey McGovern in a dream to say "Go where you will be valued." She tells Patricia Cuney "Organize four conferences: Goddess, Birth, Earth, Death."

Other women see the Goddess as a symbol or concept. For Riane Eisler, the Goddess is "a way of looking at the powers that govern our lives in a more benign way." Starr Goode sees Her as "a process of revelation." As a writer, I find it gratifying that many women mention books as pivotal to their spiritual journeys. Others encounter the Goddess through art, music, pilgrimage, or through the presence of another human being.

Over and over again, we hear the word "empowerment." However we experience the Goddess, She grounds us in love and acceptance of our bodies, challenges us to be who we fully are, and helps us find our deepest sources of courage and strength.

There are many women in this book I know personally; others whose work I know but whom I have never met. Now I feel a connection to each of them at a deeper, core level. My own choices and experiences are affirmed by seeing them reflected in this book.

The Goddess movement is maturing and growing. We are now old enough to have a second generation of children coming to adulthood who were raised in this tradition. We are faced with new challenges as we move through a new millennium—how to grow without institutionalizing ourselves, how to organize without bureaucratizing, how to solidify our visions without rigidifying our beliefs.

In the Footsteps of the Goddess is a timely gift. By presenting a spectrum of our real experiences with the Goddess, Cristina Biaggi holds up a magic mirror to the face of our movement, in which we can see our true reflection. However we think of the Goddess, we cannot read these stories without coming to believe that something is alive in the world and speaking to us. The women and men who have so honestly shared their deep soul experiences teach us that there are many ways to listen.

—*Starhawk, October 1999*

Introduction

This book is the story of my own coming to the Goddess and how this transformed my life and work as well as a compilation of Goddess stories provided by women and men from many walks of life. I met some of these people along the way; others I met through the questionnaires I sent out to collect these stories. *In the Footsteps of the Goddess* is a recording of when and how they came to this important discovery and how it affected their lives. I believe this sort of examination and telling of women's and men's stories is important, especially now, because it reveals a deep spiritual yearning which cannot be ignored.

The idea for this book came to me when I attended a women's spirituality conference in Mankato, Minnesota. I had gone to Mankato to lecture about my first book, *Habitations of the Great Goddess,* and while there I made two significant discoveries.

Because of a combination of New York and European egocentrism, I did not know that Mankato even existed, let alone that people there had been organizing Goddess conferences since 1984. I was amazed to discover that this women's spirituality gathering started with no more than twenty participants, and now boasts over 900 attendees (mostly women) who come from all over the United States. I was gratified with this discovery—maybe the "Goddess Movement" was finally making some significant progress.

My second discovery took place during a dinner conversation with five of the conference participants. As we sat around the table talking, I realized that every one of the women sitting there had undergone a profound experience which led her to the Goddess, an experience that had transformed her life. Sometimes, the discovery was triggered by a pivotal event. Sometimes the change was more gradual. One woman, who had been a housewife with five grandchildren, left a stale marriage, went back to school, and became a therapist dealing with women's issues. Another had started a library of women's books and was writing a novel based on women's spirituality. Through finding the Goddess, each woman had found herself and each had a fascinating story to tell.

I found myself inspired by these stories of transformation and self-fulfillment. I reasoned that if there were stories like this in Mankato, there had to be more stories in other parts of the United States and elsewhere. It was just a matter of conducting the right sort of search. I also felt that the exponential growth of the Mankato conference, from 20 to 900 participants in 15 years, confirmed a significant and growing interest in women's spirituality and in the Goddess movement.

I left the conference with a resolve to find more stories of transformation and collect them in a book. My purpose in sharing them is to inspire readers to do some spiritual exploration on their own, to find the personal stories that have given their lives meaning or motivated them to change direction.

I am an artist by profession—a sculptor. For over twenty years, my chief source of inspiration and focus has been the Great

Goddess in all her manifestations. I also write and lecture about the Goddess. My research, writing, and lectures are a source of inspiration for my artistic endeavors while my art nurtures my writing.

My first book, *Habitations of the Great Goddess* (Knowledge, Ideas & Trends, 1994), was an exploration of Goddess cultures on the island of Malta and on the Orkney and Shetland islands north of Scotland. Through an examination of tombs, temples, and artifacts of these ancient island cultures, I traced the beginning, the development, the apex, and the decline of the tomb and temple builders and the populations they served. By actively engaging in both endeavors—creating art inspired by the Goddess and writing about Her—I feel that I have deepened my understanding of women's spirituality, past and present. I hope the stories that follow will help you do the same.

—*Cristina Biaggi*

Acknowledgments

During the three years this book has been in the making, a number of people have helped me with its production. I would like to thank, first of all, my publisher, Sandra Brown, whose faith in this book inspired me to undertake it. My heartfelt thanks go next to my editor, Sonja Hakala, whose commitment to this project has been inspired, complete, and unwavering.

I am grateful for invaluable help from my assistant, Robin Mooring, in all the aspects of this project. She has unwaveringly rushed to my assistance whenever I had computer problems (which was all too often). My heartfelt thanks also to my friend Peter Skinner, my sister, Marina Harrison, and my partner, Patricia Walsh, for reading my manuscript at different stages. I would also like to thank my brother, Gianni Biaggi, my daughter, Diana Green, and my son, John Anderson.

However, my greatest gratitude goes to the many women and men who contributed to this book and made it possible. They are: Catherine Allport, Amejo Amyot, Eva Yaa Asantewaa, Nancy Azara, Dorothy Barenholz, Sandra Barnhouse, Suzanne Bellamy, Agathe Bennich, Kristina Berggren, Cassia Berman, Sofia Birden, Lucia Chiavola Birnbaum, Mary Brenneman, Sedonia Cahill, Dorothy Cameron, Janine Canan, Christopher, Christopher Castle, *acknowledgments*

Joan Cichon, Glenda Cloughley, Patricia Cuney, Lori DeGayner, Miriam Robbins Dexter, Isobel Dowler, Charoula Dontopoulos, Imogene Drummond, Olympia Dukakis, Gail Dunlap, Connie Dunn, Riane Eisler, Karen Ethelsdattar, Barbara Ewell, Jean Freer, Lynne Fusco, Melinda Gardiner, Hazinat Gebel, Starr Goode, Tricia Grame, Laura Suzanne Gordon, Sally Hamburger, Carol Hamoy, Barbara Harrell, Lucy Harrison, Hope Kasley Rendell Harvey, Beth Hensperger, Hera, Ubaka Hill, Mary R. Hopkins, Patricia Hubbard, Jade, Linda Johnsen, Judith Johnson, Ruth Klein, Neen Namrae Lillquist, Mimi Lobell, Katie Locke, Karen London, Ayo Maat, Elizabeth MacNabb, Tatyana Mamonova, Joan Marler, Chris Martin, Diana Marto, Linda Watanabe McFerrin, Patricia Healey McGovern, Susan Menje, Julie Forest Middleton, Vicki Noble, Gloria Orenstein, Ruth Rhoden, Len Rosenberg, Lydia Miller Ruyle, Natalie Schuette, Sylvia Sims, Monica Sjöö, Jill Smith, Edwin Chin Song, Griselda Steiner, Cheryl Straffon, Jenny Badger Sultan, Alyce Tresenfeld, Anette Van Dyke, Joya Verde, Valli Wasp, Terry Whye, Donna Wilshire, Ellen Wolfe, and Suzanne Zuckerman. I thank you all!

Chapter One

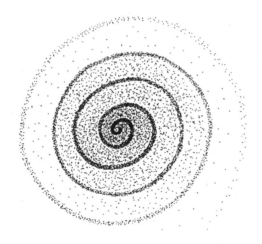

turning everything upside down:
the Goddess defined

Of course, this Goddess turns everything we have learned in the West upside down.

—*Donna Wilshire*

To me, the Goddess is the numinous manifestation of all that is and isn't. The Great Numinous doesn't necessarily need to possess one sex or the other but I feel this force as a powerful and loving female presence. Intellectually, I recognize Her as the prehistoric Great Goddess of archaeology and mythology who was paramount to our ancestors long before the advent of a great God.

—*Cristina Biaggi*

When we express compassion for others, we are the living Goddess. And that same act of love acknowledges the Goddess-self in the other person.

We are all the Goddess in many forms and many guises.

—*Susan Menje*

The Goddess is inside me, is the earth, the nurturing, the love, the connectedness, the food, air, water . . . the music and laughter . . . the joy, happiness and freedom . . . the dignity and honor in all women and the female energy in men. The Goddess is the real center of creation in many guises and has many names. She is our strength, endurance, intuition, persistence, empathy. She is mother to all the living creatures on the earth and is in the rocks, and waters of the earth. She is the light and the oneness with all.

—*Hope Kasley Rendell Harvey*

The Goddess is a friend.

—*Patricia Healey McGovern*

The Goddess is a paradigm, among other paradigms, of like-minded people working together toward a goal of universal peace, universal education, universal freedom, a race of humans together on this planet.

The Goddess gives women and some men a different perspective. She is a symbol, a living force, to carry this vision of the Earth and the new-but-old way of connecting to each other, to the life of the Earth, and all the life on the Earth. The Goddess is an energy and a mystery.

—*Starr Goode*

Bone of my bone, blood of my blood, ground of my being; the Earth on which I walk and which sustains me; the ocean I sail over and swim in and walk beside and which also sustains me; the universe in which I am an entity.

I do not "believe" in Her. Instead, I know Her without struggle, without having to suspend my questioning spirit, without a constant demand to worship Her to make Her "real." She is so worthy of my worship that She does not need it or demand it so I rejoice in worshipping Her.

—*Sylvia Sims*

I would define the Goddess as a great inner strength arising from my depths and in turn shared by others of like mind. She is an empowering force increased by the magic of women being together. Events involving her presence are very sacred, moving, and fulfilling. They seem to have a depth and power of their own far beyond the ordinary.

—*Neen Namrae Lillquist*

I define the Goddess as the Great Earth Mother—the womb of life. I have no concept of a personal God but I feel the rhythm, the pulse of the universe. Sometimes I'm in it, sometimes not. I imagine the concept of the Goddess was too elemental to endure man's (and I do mean man's) need to control and explain.

—*Sally Hamburger*

How would I define the Goddess? I smile as I contemplate this very big question. She is mystery and that is something inherently difficult, if not foolish, to attempt to define! She has been called by thousands of names—All That Is, Gaia. She comes to me in the fleeting and wild realms of dreamtime, contemplation, stillness, and ritual.

—*Terry Whye*

I don't experience Her as a being but a collection of all of our mothers, all our mothers that have ever been, and that ever will be—past, present, and future.

—*Ubaka Hill*

The Goddess is where we all begin, where we all end, and everything in between. We all come from Her, we carry with us Her spirit and energy, and then we return to Her.

—*Karen London*

The primordial Goddess represents the feminine principle rather than a personified deity who is out there independently, acting willfully in the world. She is undifferentiated. Everything is in Her as potential, and because She is so prehistoric, there are no words written about Her so She really has no name.

Imagine the differentiated Goddess as stars. Then imagine the stars as pinholes in the vault of heaven. Beyond the pinholes are the archetypes, the spirits, and the divine beings, and the stars let their intelligence and consciousness come into our world.

—*Mimi Lobell*

I always define the Goddess in Earth-based forms—mud, earth, rock, water. I approach the many phases of female divinity in very grounded forms. And in meditation, I receive a flow of language from multi-layered personas of a "Goddess" energy.

—*Suzanne Bellamy*

She is the one who nurtures, loves, and supports me as I walk the paths I have chosen in my life. The paths have been hard at times but I know that She has never left my side even as I descended into the dark night of my soul, even as I was stripped of all that I held precious in my physical life.

I have come to know Her as the One who brings life, who comforts in pain, who encourages when all hope is lost, who holds the light to show the path out of darkness, and as the One who will receive my body and soul when I pass from this life.

—*Valli Wasp*

For me, the Goddess is both a spiritual symbol that empowers women and a symbol of human possibilities. There's a cyclical unity in Her. With the Goddess, one does not structure relations in such a way that they constantly cause pain and death. Instead, one accepts that death and pain are there but one does not seek them out or glorify them or make them sacred as a way of justifying human cruelty and injustice. She symbolizes a way of looking at the powers that govern our lives in a more benign way, a less punitive way than the conventional deities that have historically come out of what I call dominator societies.

I believe that the ancient magical rites were actually more rites of alignment than rites performed to control or persuade a deity.

To try to align life-giving, life-sustaining, pleasure-giving, positive energies is a more participatory experience than performing magic to give yourself a sense of control.

—*Riane Eisler*

The Goddess is a multitude of manifestations of the divine and ordinary mysteries in a multiplicity of female forms.

—*Catherine Allport*

The Goddess is the wisdom inside us all, the wisdom inside the Earth, the wisdom found in life's unfolding processes. These—and I think all—definitions of the Goddess imply a spiritual value system that has profound consequences for cultural transformation.

—*Imogene Drummond*

The Goddess, to me, is being free to make one's own individual choices, glorying at being alive, singing and dancing praises, painting praises, living truly in one's nature.

—*Agathe Bennich*

Like most humans, I have pet names for Spirit on all levels of existence, and some of them are female names. I have a deep fondness for certain individual goddesses such as Tara, Yemaya, Ochun, and Quan Yin. We humans like to name things, including the various expressions and manifestations of Spirit that we encounter.

I believe Gaia is the dynamic spirit of life within all things existent on our Earth and the manifestation of all things existent on our Earth.

She is Earth in total and Earth is totally alive, a breathing (and suffering) organism, and everything is interconnected. There is a cosmic "Gaia" too, though I do not have a name for this level of Spirit except to call it Mystery as aboriginal people do.

Although I use it, I actually have some trouble with the official term "The Goddess." I don't think it has a gender!

—*Eva Yaa Asantewaa*

I don't actually define the Goddess. I refer to "Goddess" rather than "The Goddess." I believe Goddess is the power of Creation and Life, the Life Force from the cosmos to the tiniest atom, the inter-relationship of all life.

—*Jill Smith*

She is One. She is Many. She is the Earth and the cosmos. She is creative intelligence and beauty. She is death and decay, change and rebirth. She is in the corn and in the seed and in the stalk. She is the highest sky and the heat at noon. She is rats as well as butterflies. She is all possibility and all there is. She is Truth.

—*Gail Dunlap*

The Goddess for me is the Divine Feminine, the eternal source of becoming, declining, and renewal at all levels of Being. I have grown very conscious of the three-fold power which, to me, is the

basis of all life and is in and through all living creatures, often manifesting itself as a spiral form like our galaxy.

—Dorothy Cameron

She-Who-Is, in whose image I am. She who moves and lives in us
and all creation, whose being we live within. She shows Herself to
us in countless ways. We know Her in Her manifestations and
names in every culture. She stands with us in every aspect of our
living and dying—comes close to us in our dear ones, in our times
of birthing and loss.

—Melinda Gardiner

I see Her as a metaphor for reconnecting human to
human, human to animal, human to the Earth. I see Her
roundness—her breast/body/house—as a nurturing
source, such as our mothers' grandmothers.

—Judith Johnson

This morning, as I was watering my garden (dozens of containers
on a narrow setback, fourteen floors above the streets of
Brooklyn), I felt I was seeing the Goddess. She was present in the
riotous purple of multitudes of bobbing pansies, the annual mira-
cle of parsley, thyme, and oregano renewing themselves, the
endurance of geraniums, releafing once more after another battle
in their war for existence against the northwesterly winds that
transform my terrace into a sometimes violent mini-climate. She

is also in the wind and the hail that accompanied hour after hour of thunder and lightening which illuminated the night while I worried that these frail plants would drown or blow out to sea.

—*Suzanne Zuckerman*

Chapter Two

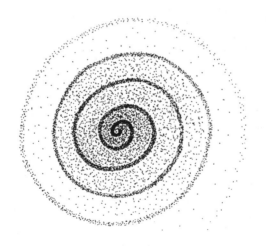

go where you are valued:
personal stories

I had no idea that God could be Mother.

—*Cassia Berman*

One of my mother's most cherished stories, which she related to me repeatedly (I loved hearing it), was the following. My mother lost her own mother when she was five years old. Early one morning, when my mother was about seven, she went out into her garden in Salt Lake City, where she lived, and, as she put it, "I saw a fairy poised on a large leaf. She was an exquisite small being with gossamer wings and transparent skirt and a perfect little body. She only lingered on the leaf for a few moments and then she darted off and I was left with a feeling of great happiness which lasted all day long. I knew everything would be all right after that."

A feeling of great happiness was conjured up whenever my Mother told me this story and when she recounted it, her face became transfigured by joy. The story always made me feel closer to her but, as time went on, I also wished that I would have such a vision to inspire me. Later on, when I "discovered" the Goddess, I began to believe that my mother had experienced a manifestation of the Female Divine. I always derived much solace from the story and it established a deep sense of connection between my mother and myself—which is perhaps why I am writing this book.

Even though I've never experienced a wonderful vision such as my mother's, I've had several significant dreams. In one dream, when I was about sixteen, I was in an apple orchard in full bloom. I was lying down, my head resting in the lap of a most beautiful woman who gazed down at my face with a look of transported joy. She was caressing my hair with her exquisitely soft hands and her beautiful face was framed by a halo of red-gold hair against a background of white apple blossoms and a deep blue sky. As we looked into each other's eyes, there was a feeling of bliss. And yet there was the understanding that I was the acolyte and that she was the numinous being—the Mother Goddess. When I woke up, I felt supremely happy and totally at peace. This dream has given me solace throughout my life and I've gone back to it in moments of extreme stress. In retrospect I feel that, even though I did not have a vision of Her as my mother had, I experienced the Female Divine in a dream.

But how did I discover the Goddess? I was brought up in the Catholic faith and had always felt something was lacking in the traditional concept of divinity. I instinctively knew there had to be something more than "God," that "God" was a later incursion, an addendum. When I was young, during the 1950s, even the Virgin Mary seemed too tied by the shackles of patriarchy to be a meaningful representative of female spirituality.

Every once in a while, I came across the words "The Goddess" in my readings and would feel an emotional and physical surge.

Then, in the early 1970s, while I was seeking a proper topic for my master's dissertation, I read these words: "In the beginning there was woman. The man appears as the son, as a biologically younger and later phenomenon. The female is the older, the more powerful, and the most aboriginal of the two mysterious, fundamental forms . . ." These words, by Helen Diner in *Mothers and Amazons,* seemed so right and powerful that they propelled me on my quest for the Goddess. My mind, my whole being, became consumed with the desire to read, to learn as much as possible about this spiritual force.

I began to systematically consume the few tomes then available on the Goddess, books by Jane Harrison, Robert Briffault, Johann Bachofen, E. O. James, and Joseph Campbell. Then I discovered the work of Marija Gimbutas. She claimed that worship of the Goddess was universal during the Paleolithic and early Neolithic periods throughout Europe and in many parts of Asia and the Eastern Mediterranean. I realized that while the other writers talked about the Goddess as a peripherally numinous force, Gimbutas placed Her at center stage—she claimed the Goddess was the first spiritual force in the lives of ancient human beings.

During this period of time, I also read Merlin Stone's *When God Was a Woman* and Michael Dames's *The Silbury Treasure* in which he sets forth the idea of Neolithic temple and tombs as representing the Goddess's body as a place to be entered.

I completed my master's degree and embarked on my Ph.D. I used parts of my dissertation, "Megalithic Sculptures That Symbolize the Great Goddess," to write my first book, *Habitations of the Great Goddess.* My thesis included a sculptural project, "The GG Sculpture," which consists of a double-shelled papier-mâché construction on a wood and wire armature. On the outside, this piece measures approximately 24 x 14 feet and is 8½ feet high. On the inside, it is 18 x 8½ feet and is 6½ feet high. The sculpture represents a reclining female figure (the Great Goddess), six times life-size, lying on her side, her arm resting along her hip, her legs disappearing into the Earth below her knees. The figure is concealed by an outside structure which has the appearance of an irregular buff-colored rock with rounded sides and top. The amorphous rock-like outside conceals the negative-space image of the figure within, thus adding to the mystery and numinous quality of the experience of entering the sculpture. A recessed, red, oval doorway leading into the figure's interior is positioned on the outside. The position of this doorway, corresponding to the figure's navel on the inside, is important. Our navels have been our connecting links to our Mother since the beginning of time.

This piece was meant to be an experimental mock-up, the first of a series of large outdoor sculptures focusing on internal space—the body of the Great Goddess. The inspirations for this piece were the megalithic monuments from the Neolithic period which I studied and discussed in my dissertation and book.

After I completed my dissertation and its accompanying sculpture, I joined a Goddess group in New York. About ten of us met once a month to discuss our work and to exchange valuable information. Several of us were writing books about the Goddess. After we had been meeting for about two years, we decided to go on a field trip. Our timing could not have been better. A conference on ancient religions in the Mediterranean—"*The Archaeology and Fertility Cult in the Mediterranean*"—was scheduled for the same time and it was to be held in Malta. Eight of us went to the conference and three of us gave papers. It was there that I met Marija Gimbutas.

We participated in the conference with Marija and other archaeologists, among them Colin Renfrew and David Trump. We all enjoyed wonderful dinners under the stars, field trips, and free-for-all discussions. Catherine Allport and I taped interviews with Marija and organized and taped a debate between Colin and Marija. In addition to this, I made arrangements in advance with the Director of Antiquities at the Archaeological Museum in Valletta, Malta to have exclusive access to the limestone-carved subterranean Hypogeum for two hours to perform a ritual. Since this structure had only been rediscovered in 1904, this was perhaps the first time since the Third Millennium B.C.E.., when the Hypogeum was still in use as a tomb and place of worship, that a ritual by women had been conducted in its dark womb-like depths.

Mimi Lobell, one of the respondents in this book, wrote the following vivid description of our ritual, which she read at Marija Gimbutas's memorial service on May 7, 1994.

We entered the Hypogeum via the basement of a plain little building on a narrow street in the town of Hal Saflieni. While we waited in the cool cavern for the tourists and the guard to leave, we explored its three-dimensional, multi-level labyrinth of chambers. Finally we were alone— Catherine Allport, Cristina Biaggi, Virginia Dare, Charoula [Dontopoulos], Gail Dunlap, Joya Frye, Marija Gimbutas,

Buffie Johnson, Patricia Reis, and myself. We ran around freely, revivifying the sacred Neolithic womb-cavern with our reverent enthusiasm, admiring the fine stonework in the holy-of-holies, marveling at the ancient red pomegranates painted on the ceiling (one conference scholar had presented the Hypogeum as the earliest known sacred site of Demeter and Persephone), and sounding into the oracle holes to disprove an old local saying that only a man's voice would carry properly. We placed lit candles and incense in niches and on ledges. We smudged and anointed one another. We called out the names of the Goddess, and evoked members of our group who couldn't be there. As many Goddess-women are wont to do, some stripped down— Virginia halfway, Catherine all the way. We brought out our music makers, and sang and chanted and danced to the Goddess in high spirits. We passed around little gifts—fine spiral shells Charoula had gathered at one of the temples, feathers I had found on Queen Maeve's mound in Ireland. We each said something profound, and sent healing energies out to the Earth and all her life-forms. We joined hands and circled, again and again. Marija was thoroughly enjoying all of this. As we circled, we invited her into the center to incarnate the Goddess. With no hesitation, she moved immediately to the center of the circle, the center of the Hypogeum, the center of the Goddess realm beyond space and time. She knelt down and looked up, her face radiant, her eyes distant. 'Who are you?' we asked. 'I am the Goddess,' she said, and then she went on for a few minutes in an oracular voice. As far as I know, none of us remembers exactly what she said. But the message was one of abundant unconditional love and ever-flowing life energy, and boundless creativity and regeneration, and eternal wisdom and peace.

The ritual was so powerful that a day later, three post-menopausal women in our group menstruated.

—*Cristina Biaggi*

Because my father's father was deeply religious, we were members of an Orthodox synagogue until my brother had his bar mitzvah. I attended Saturday children's services and classes in the phonetics of Hebrew for prayer. I understood God as the primary author of a lot of inexplicable rules. After the bar mitzvah, we joined a Reform temple where I attended Sunday classes in Jewish historic culture. God, the very personal confidante of the charismatic, silver-maned chief rabbi, was rarely mentioned.

I had a private religion that was instilled by my mother. She told me what her grandmother had told her: *God is always watching.* This often-repeated statement created an intimate relationship in which my God was concerned with clean underwear, nose picking, and petty acts of revenge. It was clear that this ever-observant and negatively critical being neither noticed nor disapproved of the unfairness, cruelty, and spite of my peers. Only I was special enough to draw God's continuous scrutiny with its implied expectations of punishment and reward.

I think the Goddess discovered me. Although I had extensive education in religion and mythology, Goddess information was presented intellectually either as engaging fiction or as historical explanations for the obligatory activities of American culture and Judaism. I had no sense that this material could represent anything of a positive, personal nature.

My awareness has grown through daily meditation, reading, participation in spiritual groups, and personal experience with Goddess-powered objects and sites of reverence to Her. There was no specific moment when my sense of self in relation to the universe evolved. But it is this connection that I consider my discovery of the Goddess.

My early life was overshadowed by fears of punishment meted out by a ubiquitous, capricious, and vengeful God. Growing older, I developed the intellectual awareness that the God of my childhood was absurd and I became pseudo-agnostic in my beliefs. But the emotional paranoia and the habits that accompanied that childhood experience remained. It was only after visceral experiences of the Goddess that my consciousness shifted.

During a meditation, I saw Her incarnated as a radiant brunette, bending over me and looking deep into my psyche. Terrified, I stopped breathing while memories of my negative acts flowed in a cinematic montage that blocked my view of Her. She laughed. The images shattered. I inhaled and felt bathed in love that extended universally.

The consequence of the change in my perception of deity is that instead of attempting to fulfill the unknowable expectations of an external God, I merely have to be aware of and responsible for my own actions. This is both a relief and an empowerment. In terms of day-to-day action, I am able to work in an environment of extreme hostility where insults pass for conversation and violence has no consequences. [Suzanne is a special education teacher in a New York City vocational high school.] I do so without feeling threatened because I see the Goddess energy in each of the people I encounter there. I know that when I am totally-from-my-heart-honest and not using truth as a weapon, I am heard and understood.

Each day brings me new connections, new awareness, and new reasons to be grateful to the Goddess. For example, after many disappointing dates for which I had spent lots of time preparing, it occurred to me that my disappointment was proportional to my preparation. In merchandising myself, I had made it my date's responsibility to amuse or inform me enough to equal the value at which I had mentally priced my preparatory efforts. One evening, as I prepared to go out, I thought about this in relation to how I prepare to meditate, visit with the Goddess. If I am able to participate in this central life relationship in comfortable clothes, I thought, surely I can do the same with a stranger. My subsequent dates have actually proved to be far more amusing, informative, and pleasant.

—*Suzanne Zuckerman*

Strangely enough, I discovered the Goddess in my teens. It was my intimate secret. I only told my girlfriend. I was writing poetry to the Goddess (She looked more like a beautiful Greek goddess then) and I was whispering these poems to Her like prayers before falling asleep.

I was born in Russia, where a mixture of paganism and Christianity is pretty typical. I was able to combine my developing philosophy of life from the best of Slavic paganism (our goddess Lada, for example, is well known as a protectress) and Christianity in its pure form (compassion, not violence), avoiding any fanaticism. Both traditions taught me wisdom and good. After my exile to the west, I was impressed with *The First Sex,* by Elizabeth Davis, and *The Chalice and the Blade,* by Riane Eisler.

—*Tatyana Mamonova*

The Goddess, in her crone manifestation, came to me in a dream. I had returned to college as a part-time student and was at a crossroads. I was struggling to decide whether to stay with my career, choose a major and remain a part-time student, or accept a grant to attend Vassar College full-time.

The Goddess appeared to guide me and give me strength. Her message was to "go where you are valued." And I did. I received so much positive feedback at Vassar College, my self-esteem grew exponentially with the amount of time I spent there. I chose to leave my career and attend full-time.

Before the Goddess, I had been spiritually bereft and She filled the spiritual void. I discovered that Mary, Mother of Jesus, had strong connections to the Goddess and I developed a new appreciation of Her.

Why did She appear at that time? I had opened myself up to new ideas and thoughts, new possibilities. I was struggling, and I needed Her. She came because She knew I would embrace Her.

My personal life took on a totally different shape. I moved from a victim stance to the attitude that I am the creator of my destiny. I became assertive, independent, and selective in my tasks. I removed the chains and became a free spirit. My marriage suffered and I am now divorced. I gave up the "can't do" and substituted "can do."

I became a writer, what I was meant to be. I believe very strongly in service but realize that service takes many forms and that writing is my manner of service.

—*Patricia Healey McGovern*

Let me preface this by saying I didn't use psychedelics to the extent many in my generation did. But the first time I took peyote, Midsummer's Night 1978, I heard a gentle female voice inside me say, "These are your hands." She proceeded to introduce me to myself from inside, step by step. I was with a friend who had been trying for months to interest me in Sri Ramakrishna and the Divine Mother tradition of India. When I told him what was happening inside, he took out a picture of Sri Sarada Devi, Ramakrishna's spiritual partner, who is believed to be a full incarnation of the Goddess, and told me I had a connection with her.

I was 29 when I had that experience and had been calling to God to speak to me for many years, but I had no idea that God could be Mother. My own father died when I was very young and I always looked for my father in every situation. On the other hand, I had a difficult relationship with my mother, who loved me but was possessive and controlling. The last thing I would have said I needed was a "Mother."

My life changed direction completely. I had been living a pretty wild and confused life in Manhattan, a life which was not bringing me any real satisfaction. I had to be weaned away from New York City, which I thought was the center of the universe, and change the purpose of my life. [Cassia is a poet, and had been teaching, publishing, and giving poetry readings in the New York art world.] I became more sensitive to the noise, smells, energies of New York and the city became an affront to my life force. I moved to the country, a relocation I've never regretted.

I gradually realized I had been raised to betray my life force in many ways, and had become callous towards it. "Purity" had not been part of my vocabulary but over the years that's where She's been taking me. I stopped smoking cigarettes spontaneously when I moved to the country and had better air to breathe. She instructed me from within not to use drugs or alcohol so that I could perceive Her in every ordinary moment. I also had to "change my mind"—cease finding satisfaction in negative thoughts, release negative feelings toward others, reexamine and simplify my desires, and cultivate a peace I had no idea was possible.

I lost my taste for meat and became a vegetarian. Over the years, I've realized there are very good reasons to be a vegetarian because if you honor life, you don't want to kill life. Becoming a vegetarian sensitized me to the shameful way the meat and dairy industries treat living creatures, to the way the food industry mistreats the Earth, and to the way we mistreat our bodies.

I realized I couldn't be sexually promiscuous. I started

to feel the ramifications of taking the essence and vibrations of a man into my body, and realized it wasn't something to do lightly.

As I've become more and more pure about what I put into my body, it makes it difficult to live in this culture. I'm constantly being shown how to further respect and revere life, and it takes me a while to let go of the carelessness which is so common, and take time, for example, to commune with the living essence of food (my current lesson).

As I became drawn into Her love, I began to pray for a female teacher, and within a couple of years She led me to a wonderful one, the late Hilda Charlton, who taught me what it means to walk a spiritual path. I moved to the country the year I met Hilda and my spiritual life became very intense and dedicated. For some years I ceased to have a public life and turned inward to learn how to see myself and let go of old habits that kept me from the light. Over the last twenty years, I've found that the need to withdraw comes and goes—sometimes I'm called upon to go very deep within and then I come to a point when I have to go out and work in the world with what I've learned. The Divine Mother rules my life, and did even before I was aware of Her. I feel I can trust Her completely because I've always had what I need. She's never let me down even though my life certainly hasn't gone the way I thought it would.

I've never been able to make plans. When I do, they rarely amount to anything. But She has arranged my life so that things happen that I didn't even know about. How do I know this is the doing of the Goddess? Because the wonderful events in my life generally have to do with Her—being in company that honors Her, being given opportunities to serve Her through writing or teaching. All of these events bear Her name in one way or another, and bring me a joy and sense of security and peace that even after all these years is still mysterious.

Since discovering the Goddess, it's been a very long and gradual path—letting go of ego, turning away from appearances, and learning to live and perceive from my inner self. Although I was never sold on this society to begin with, I'd say my values are very different from what they were. I'm stronger and more confident in who I am, which is dependent on Her. I have to do my part, but how successful my efforts are depends on how totally I surrender each moment to Her—and that success cannot be measured by worldly appearances.

—*Cassia Berman*

My experience was merely discovering the Goddess within and melting into Maat, the Egyptian Goddess, the One who weighs the heart on the scale of truth, brings order where there is chaos, and represents balance.

My diet and lifestyle changed naturally. I stopped smoking, drinking, going to discos; I changed my dress. I was happy, less focused on materialism, but felt taken care of. I was being healed from past marital failures and the abuse from my second husband.

—*Ayo Maat*

As a male artist incorporating Goddess iconography into my work, I am often asked how I came to be so deeply involved with this feminine imagery. As an art student in England, I was particularly interested in the mysteries of the land of ancient Britain and, with a group of like-minded friends, began to study the layers of history and the patterns of consciousness written into the landscape. Gradually I became aware of the Goddess as a recurring image within Neolithic cosmology. In turn, the implications of this pervasive Goddess idea reached into my life and touched me profoundly.

The Goddess emerged not simply from the feminine energy that I love so much in women but in my own heart and sense of androgyny. Within my own body, I felt the ebb and flow of energies both male and female. Being a man, I felt the masculine drive yet it was always moderated by an empathetic sense of the yielding within myself. The Earth seems to me to be the mother of this experience, manifesting the same dynamic.

My study of Goddess imagery from prehistory and the art that I created as a result brought me into contact with many artists, writers, and thinkers walking a similar path. Almost all have been women. I think there are plenty of men who have similar experiences but do not wish to be seen as associated with a Goddess movement. There may be reasons for their fears but I don't know them. I find I have been graciously accepted by the many women who might otherwise have rejected the possibility that men could experience the kind of redemption they consider appropriate.

I don't think my philosophy of life changed as a result of my "discovery" of the Goddess. I see the concept of Goddess as something I always knew and felt but simply had not named.

—*Christopher Castle*

Despite my family's deep religious background, I describe my early religious experience as someone who is vaccinated but it does not "take." I found Christianity to be a strange religion and could never understand its appeal. For years, this was a secret I kept, thinking the whole "civilized" world was Christian. But in a sociology class during my last year in high school, I finally understood there were millions of people who were not Christian. I was relieved. I began to look for a religion or spirituality which suited my beliefs. For a while I was an atheist, then an agnostic until finally, at age 25, I encountered Goddess religion.

At first I resisted accepting the notion of Goddess. I did not embrace the idea of God and the Goddess looked too much like God. I felt that you can't dress God in a skirt (in drag) and assume I wouldn't know Him. The Goddess, however, seeped into my consciousness. I started reading books which described matrifocal societies, religious traditions, and culture. They helped me conceptualize the changes which take place in a culture when divinity is viewed as exclusively male. I came to believe that the religions of these cultures had been suppressed and became what we have been taught today to call witchcraft.

Eight years after first encountering the Goddess, I cofounded the Re-formed Congregation of the Goddess. The Congregation currently has over 1,000 members, all of whom are women from locations all over North America. I am employed by the

Congregation as its priestess, administrator, and general visionary. My duties include copublishing the oldest women's spirituality newspaper in the country, *Of a Like Mind,* teaching, and administering the Women's Theological Institute which, through its Cella programs, trains women in leadership development and priestessing (ministerial duties).

I found that knowledge gained from intuitive sources was accepted in both matrifocal cultures and the Craft. I learned that the Goddess was not God in drag but a deity who brought with Her a different consciousness and approach to life. I began to realize how many of the concepts of traditional religion had been twisted and/or stolen from Goddess religion. And, finally, I understood that the Goddess was what I had been looking for all along.

My acceptance of the Goddess had a profound impact on my life. I felt compelled to use the organizational skills gained from working as an executive director of a nonprofit organization to provide services to the Goddess community. After being inspired by my experience at a Goddess conference, I told the women with whom I had traveled that if only I had a little money, I knew ways to organize for the Goddess.

When I arrived home, the phone was ringing. It was my mother calling to tell me that my grandmother, with whom I had had a serious values conflict, had died and left me a 3.5-carat diamond ring, a mink coat, and some nuclear power plant stock. I took the sudden appearance of "a little money" as confirmation that my intention to organize had merit. From that point on, the Goddess has been a primary focus of my life and work.

—Jade

From the time I was a child, I had the feeling that there was something wrong with me. The world I saw and experienced was not what the authors of the great books or the preachers of the great religions described as true and good. Eventually I stopped trying to make sense out of what I was told because it was clear to me that I didn't get it. I was different, inadequate, deficient in my ability to understand what "they" were talking about.

Of course, this realization brought me great sadness and eventually a sense of self-loathing, even despair. Imagine my joy when I discovered that my perceptions were not unique, that there were countless people who shared my observations about life and Nature, and that the strangeness I felt was because my female body and my female experience did not resemble the western "Ideal" which has long been "Man."

When I first heard about the Goddess of prehistory, I felt a surge of renewed interest in the world which led me to a confidence in myself and a sense of worthiness. Learning about the Goddess was for me a great homecoming experience, a welcoming feeling of being embraced by reality instead of being rejected by it.

I am not really a new woman for having found the Goddess as a model of being. In many ways I am the same—it's my attitude that's different. Now I am happy to be me, proud of myself and my womanhood. I am fully authorized, full of potential and goodness, intimately hooked into the Life Force that teems with everything. No longer feeling inadequate because of my female perceptions and womanly desires, I think of myself as a worthy daughter and deserving heiress of my Mother's gifts.

—*Donna Wilshire*

Epiphany, now that's a subject I can tell you about. I've had many of them during the past few years. An epiphany is when, for just a moment or two, everything comes together. In that fleeting time, it's possible to comprehend a huge amount of wisdom, or to understand on very deep levels not normally open to consciousness how the world is, what is happening or has happened. I first experienced this when I was going to college during the mid-1960s.

I grew up religious, going to church in various Protestant churches—usually the one that was close by—but left them either because my family moved or because I couldn't agree with the church. While a freshman in college, I joined the Mormon church, partly because of the influence of my uncle, who married into the church, but also because of their very slick, very effective missionary lessons. I really bought it.

In the early 1960s, I also sympathized with the Civil Rights movement, and when, after approximately six months of membership as a Mormon, I learned that African-Americans weren't allowed to hold the higher priesthood, I was horrified. I also found myself torn between my love of history as I'd begun to learn it from my secular professors, and the Mormon view of history, which I experienced as skewed to fit their eschatology. I couldn't see a place in my future as a Mormon where I could still read the history of the world and believe it as I saw it.

I was young, naive, and had no way to verbalize these conflicts. All I knew by the summer of 1965 was that I didn't fit in among the Mormons, and I couldn't go back to being a Protestant.

After an unfinished semester as a sophomore at Brigham Young University, I returned to my original school in Colorado to study art education. While attending summer school, I discovered I liked to go to a place near the campus that was semi-wild, a grove of cottonwoods set on a ridge next to a cornfield. I liked the sound of the trees there and I frequently went to this spot to be alone.

One afternoon, I sat down against one of the huge trees just to listen. Because I'd been torn about my status with the Mormons, and because I was still thinking about religious questions, my mind wandered to thoughts of mortality. This seemed to me to be one of the major questions I should be able to ask a religion to deal with. I had begun to take pride in my body, and I was thinking what a shame it had to get old and die. I thought randomly about this for a while, and then recalled a film I'd seen in a biology class, studying a spot of land in Canada. The filmmaker had set up the camera in the same location over a ten year period and recorded the changes that happened over time.

The first year, several bodies of dead elk were beginning to go back into the ground. The second year, piles of white bones lay where the elk had fallen. In the third year, the bones were widely scattered and fewer in number. By the fourth year, the bones were nearly gone. By the ninth and tenth years, the places where the elk had fallen were greener with grass that was taller than the surrounding grass. By the end of the film, those same areas had given birth to large clusters of wildflowers. The nutrients from the elk had turned to flowers. Those atoms had simply found a new home, transformed.

Thinking of this, I was overcome. I was looking out at the field at the time, saw corn growing and understood that my body could some day be corn, or one of those wonderful trees, or it might turn to wildflowers. This realization gave me sudden, exhilarating chills and tears. I was caught up in a great emotion and I saw all my atoms moving and transforming through the universe, over and over, becoming something else, and then something else again, forever.

I don't know how long this moment lasted—probably only for a few minutes. I recall the wind coming up and the trees rustling. I stood up and walked to the edge of the cornfield, all the time crying, feeling this incredible joy, chills gripping my body.

For many years, I couldn't explain why this understanding gave me a great sense of peace. But surely, as they describe the after-effects of the experience at Eleusis, I "no longer feared death."

I've since realized that I was being made aware of older, deeper indigenous memories of an earlier time. I'm still in awe that I came to that awareness in the way it happened, alone in a cottonwood grove in what now seems like another lifetime.

—*Sandra Barnhouse*

I am a painter who has been keeping a dream journal for over 30 years. In one of my dreams, a group of friends and I were building a Scythian temple in the desert. When we finished, we gathered inside for a large circle dance, all joining hands. After the dance, I wandered around alone, looking at the details of the interior. On the floor, I saw a painting and these words: "Little St. Bridget was bound so hard that when they released her, she flew."

This was such a healing image for my own life because I had felt extremely bound and constrained as a child and young person. Moreover, it seemed an image of hope for all women who have suffered so much from the bindings of patriarchy. And it also seemed to be a symbol of the hope of the release of Goddess energies which have been suppressed for such a long time. Much later, I discovered that the Irish St. Bridget had established her cell in the trunk of an oak tree that had been a shrine to the Mother Goddess, Brigid. The Irish Brigid was a triple Goddess to whom fire and the hearth were sacred. St. Bridget's nuns tended a sacred flame.

Over time, I felt the reality of the Goddess as a spiritual presence. This was very important because I felt a void when I left Christianity. I am not part of any religious group—that doesn't seem to work for me—but I do need to have a relationship to spirit. Also, it's very important to me to paint Goddess images and experiences which come to me so that I and others can be strengthened by them.

—*Jenny Badger Sultan*

At various junctures, the Goddess calls me to show me a new path. The most recent transformational experience has been the death of my mother. She had a cerebral hemorrhage. She was 84 years old and lived an active life so her sudden death was a shock and I am still dealing with it. It seems one is never quite ready to say good-bye to one's mother.

I found grief, like other emotions, must be expressed and shared. My haven has been my art. I took photographs of my mother hooked up to machines, when she died, and in the mortuary. I also took photos of myself as I cried, wailed, and grieved. I used these to create monoprint self-portraits. It helped me with letting go and healing.

—Lydia Miller Ruyle

One morning, I awakened sitting upright in my bed. As I became conscious, I remember a woman's voice saying "Your task is to organize four conferences: Goddess, Birth, Earth, and Death." I think there was more but I didn't remember it. I didn't know there was a women's spirituality movement at the time. I was not "into" the Goddess.

Several months after this, a woman named Mary gave me a copy of *Jambalaya* and inside the author, Luisa Teish, had written "To Mary, in WomanSpirit." I thought WomanSpirit was a great name and promptly organized a non-profit with that title. I didn't know that a magazine of the same name had been in existence for ten years, that there were already a number of organizations in the U.S. with that name, and that an international movement already existed.

In my regular column for the *Austin Chronicle,* I invited people to help create a conference called "The Return of the Goddess." It now seems bizarre that when it was suggested we get Z

Budapest as our speaker, I said "Who?" I have never been sure who was wackier—me with the voice, or the other women who heard my story and decided to help or join me. But 200 people came to that conference, Z Budapest spoke, and many of our lives were changed forever. Betty Sue Flowers, a professor at the University of Texas-Austin and the editor of the Joseph Campbell tapes, gave the keynote speech. The lives that were not affected by Z were changed by Betty Sue. Some of us were inspired by both. I was.

In the second conference, "Creation: Fire from the Womb," I realized in the middle of the luncheon that we were about $10,000 in debt with no possible way out. I had a dazzling moment of incredulity that I had made such a huge mistake and cost overrun. I thought of telling the attendees and asking for help but years of dealing with the internalized oppression of woman had taught me that I would be strung up by my thumbs for what I had done.

Suddenly, as I sat there contemplating the mess I had made, this energy just shot up from deep within my body, ran into some sort of encrustation at the level of my heart, and then I had a sensation of it just busting through and up, exploding pieces of "stuff," and tearing out the top of my head. I was absolutely clear in that moment that what I had done was exactly right, there was no mistake. In fact, I understood that if I had to wash dishes at that hotel for the rest of my life, it was worth it. I also realized, for the first time, that I had been in some sort of trance ever since I first heard the voice eighteen months before.

With that understanding, I asked the group for $3,500. With the support of guest speaker Judy Chicago, I raised another $1,500 through an auction at the event, raised another $1,500 through an event after the conference, and was finally bailed out of the remainder by Genevieve Vaughan, builder of the "Temple to Sekhmet" in the Nevada desert. Genevieve later employed me to coordinate the Stonehaven Goddess Program for the Foundation for a Compassionate Society, which she founded. I became one of the few full-time priestesses in the country.

What I have come to understand and believe is that She is talking to many people these days, women and men. I believe She needs our conscious collaboration and is calling out for it, even directing us. I know it is real. I just wish more women felt empowered to act when called. "Just doing it" transformed me, changed the lives of everyone around me, and rippled into the lives of 2,000 people after that. And I continue to transform—and so do they!

Two years ago I heard Her speak to me again. I was driving and meditating. She said, "It's time to go to law school." I got it together. I completed the Priestess training program of the Re-formed Congregation of the Goddess, received my credentials as a Mistress of Wicca and a member of the clergy, and started law school.

I believe in magic. I have attained faith.

—Patricia Cuney

I attended a Goddess conference at a beautiful spot in Los Angeles, in Temescal Canyon. After one of the sessions, I walked over to a creek and stood watching the coursing waters and it occurred to me that they were alive—and female. From that time, the Goddess has been an important part of my life, spiritually as well as academically. I believe that She appeared to me at this time because my work needed to change, to become more personal, and because my mother would die just a couple of years later, and I needed the sense of the female divine in order to sustain me.

—*Miriam Robbins Dexter*

My journey to the Goddess has been a gift in itself! When I unexpectedly found myself pregnant with my second child, I was not happy. Although I was (and continue to be) in a good and very satisfying marriage, my first delivery had been literally taken away from me. It was very medicated and highly technical. My son was ultimately born by cesarean section.

When I got over the shock of being pregnant this second time, I consciously embarked on a plan to "own" this pregnancy and birth. (It is important to know that my profession is nursing with a specialty in labor and birth as well as childbirth education.) I sought out the care of certified nurse-midwives. I visualized a healthy, beautiful "diva" swimming in crystal clear amniotic fluid. I visualized a labor and birth that would happen "in and through" me and not "to" me.

Although I was "surrounded" at the birth of my daughter Hannah, I was actually alone with the Goddess and, of course, my daughter. I experienced a power I was unfamiliar with (my own) and a joy beyond description. My labor lasted four hours and was the starting point of my transformation. But I didn't know it . . . yet!!

Two years later, through a series of unusual and unexpected events, I was asked to establish a women's resource center in a Catholic hospital. The center was to have a women's library. Because I had no idea how or where to begin, I contacted the local feminist bookstore. I didn't know what I was purchasing, but books like *The Spiral Dance, The Chalice and the Blade,* and *Habitations of the Great Goddess* entered my center and my life. Now I knew the Goddess and in discovering Her, I began to discover myself.

If it had been possible, I would have walked away from life as I knew it, and taken a year or two to devour books, attend women's gatherings, meditate, sing, dance bare-breasted, plan a different course for the second half of my life, and set off on a journey. Instead I have carefully, within the constraints of my already established lifestyle, worked to incorporate the Goddess into my life in a way that is meaningful to me and not threatening to my family.

I am no longer the woman my husband married; I am different all around. After four years of attempting to incorporate the Goddess into my women's center and the Catholic church, I resigned my position, returned to nursing part-time and school full-time to pursue a degree in women's studies.

The changes continue. I suspect that my role is to help other women at midlife who discover the Goddess, to help them integrate Her into lives that are already full.

—*Karen London*

I came to Goddess during the time I was a radical feminist. We wanted to do away with male dominance in every other sphere of life so it became obvious that religious and spiritual life was not exempt from this challenge. I came to Goddess because I like ritual and I like being out of doors and the pagan faith was the only one that practiced like this.

I didn't begin to understand Goddess as a spiritual force until some years after my 1971 initiation. I took up Buddhist meditation about that time, and this prepared me for what came later.

In the early 1980s, I was asked to train priestesses for the Matriarch Network in England. Through this work, I began leading regular rituals and came to understand Her power in my life. I had always been psychic but now there was a spiritual context for this power. I believe Goddess came to me because I was meant to carry a message of the Four-Fold Goddess, a message which is beyond her triple (and bare-breasted) identity. I was also to teach the importance of meditation and grounding along with raising power and making change. In a complete ritual, inner alchemy is as important as outer manifestation, and endings receive as much careful attention as beginnings.

I became a publicly practicing Dianic priestess for many years, making political alliances with other pagan groups. I trained priestesses, wrote for matriarch/Goddess/pagan and environmental publications, led public rituals, and appeared on television and radio explaining Goddess religion to non-believers. I practiced healing and prophecy and did my best to use my power and authority responsibly. I did a lot of living on the land during this time, which was absolutely wonderful.

I was the priestess who was called to Greenham Common Womyn's Peace Camp to define the use of a piece of land I named "sanctuary"—a place kept for ritual and reflection. I also had the honor of being priestess in residence at Marija Gimbutas's home in Topanga, California for the last two years of her life.

For approximately 15 years, I felt I had a mission. And then it felt as if it was over. I had not done as well as I'd hoped but the best I could do. At first, I thought the power had deserted me, but then I came to understand that it was manifesting in more private and personal ways. My era of public service was over.

—*Jean Freer*

I was 14 years old, walking across the dining room, when without warning, my awareness was no longer confined to my body. I don't mean this metaphorically, I mean it literally. I experienced myself as limitless, ecstatic consciousness pervading everything. It was the most thrilling moment of my life. Then suddenly "Linda Johnsen" realized "she" was disappearing, merging ecstatically with an ocean of all-pervading consciousness. With a shock, "I" collapsed back into "my" body—an utterly shattering experience.

Why did Divine Mother come to me at that time? I was an intensely religious, prayerful child. Each night from earliest childhood, I used to enter a state of lucid clarity high in my brain, believing that somehow, when I was in that state, I was directly in contact with God. As a fundamentalist Christian, I knew absolutely nothing about yoga or meditation, but looking back I believe that years of cultivating that state somehow triggered my mystical experience. But it would be another two years before I discovered the *Upanishads* and realized there were other people who'd had experiences like mine. I learned that in India, yogis and yoginis call this experience *pratyabhijna* (self-recognition) or *Shakti pata* (the blessing of the Goddess).

Nothing in my experience or in Christian theology had prepared me for what happened when I was 14. It was as unexpected and mind blasting as if the Earth's axis had shifted. I could no longer accept that "divine being" and "my being" were separate, or that the "external" reality beyond the confines of my skin and the "internal" reality my nervous system has direct access to are two separate realities. In the most lucid moment of my life, I had experienced them as a bliss–filled, seamless, self-aware whole.

Well, folks, it happened once but never again! The rest of my life has been a quest to return to that unitary state. I'm living a great detective story looking for clues in scriptures, accounts from mystics of many different traditions, unexpected scientific findings, philosophy, books, life experiences, and guru figures. Meditation, devotion, loving relationships, and great poetry all provide transport to wonderful altered states but Mother still hasn't picked me up and placed me back in Her lap. That one hit of the fullness of Her being was a tease. "Come and find me," She says. It's all Her game.

A year and a half ago, my husband was diagnosed with terminal bone cancer. It was totally Kali-esque, the Divine Mother tearing out my heart to draw me closer to Her. I was trying to remember a mantra to Kali which Shri Maa (one of the Shakta saints we had traveled with in Bengal and a devotee of Kali) used to repeat. My husband remembered the mantra instantly and spoke it out loud. Before he reached the last syllable, the phone rang. It was Shri Maa. We found out later that two days before she called us, Shri Maa had canceled the remainder of her Indian tour in order to fly to northern California. The first thing she did when she arrived was call Johnathan.

The next day, Shri Maa, one of the greatest women masters of northeastern India, came to our home in Sonoma and blessed Johnathan, singing *bhajans* to the Divine Mother. She assigned us both healing rituals to perform and mantras to repeat. A few days later, our doctor called. He had just gotten the final test results. All previous tests, reviewed by the entire oncology team, had shown that Johnathan had an untreatable form of malignant bone cancer. This last test contradicted all the others—it was still cancer but a form of cancer they could treat. The doctor said he absolutely couldn't understand it—they'd never seen a diagnosis change like this before. Well, he hadn't dealt with Shri Maa before.

For now, Johnathan appears to be cancer free. Yet I'm increasingly aware of the extraordinary dream-like quality of life, and of how much every breath of ours depends on Mother's will and grace.

—Linda Johnsen

I didn't really have one particular "Aha!" or what I call a Buddha moment with the Goddess. My experience was a constant unfolding. About ten years ago, She became an awareness, very, very clear, very up front, more manifested in my being. I was visiting with a therapist, speaking to her about my mother, from whom I am estranged. The therapist and I talked about the void, about the emptiness, about the lack of the mother principle in my life. And then the therapist said to me, "Have you ever thought about relating to the Goddess as your Mother." That was an "Aha!" for me that immediately filled up the void.

There's been a constant unfolding of the Goddess in all my experiences—in healing circles, with my work as a performer, when women and men reflect back to me the experience they have with me. Certainly in relationship to the drum—anywhere and everywhere, I go with the drum. Drums are connected to our hearts and the heart of the Great Mother. It constantly shows up for me in that way.

A lot of Western-minded men have this myth about women and drums, that women shouldn't play drums. But men cannot people the planet, only women can do that. So every human being on the planet comes through the womb of the Mother, of woman, and therefore every single human being ever born on Planet Earth experienced the first drum, the first pulse, the first rhythm, the first thump through the heart of a woman.

So I am working to bring the drum back to women and it's made my purpose and my relationship to the Goddess clearer.

—*Ubaka Hill*

I have known all my life that I am adopted. When I turned 21 years old, I wrote to the department of vital statistics in Illinois to get the name of my birth mother because I had been raised to believe she was dead. Soon I received a letter from someone who had looked into some files they were not supposed to in order to send me my mother's name. That person also sent me a notice saying my birth mother was not dead. Imagine the shock. *

For 24 years, I tried to find her but to no avail. Then I rewrote the place that I was adopted from, the Cradle, and they said I was born in a Salvation Army hospital.

When I spoke to the woman in charge of birth records at the Salvation Army hospital, she pulled my name up on microfilm and then found on her computer a birth that happened in 1945. Within two weeks, she had found my mother but would not tell me where she was. We adoptees have no rights to any information about our births. This woman told me to write her a letter and enclose pictures of myself. I did and she contacted my birth mother. She replied that she did not want contact but would accept the letter and pictures. I was crushed.

Then I got my own computer. Within four months I located someone who would find my mother's address for $100. I sent the money; she sent the address. I found out I had aunts and an uncle. I knew my birth mother had two sons, my half brothers, and I knew her phone number—but I was not ready for voice contact. I called the Salvation Army and told them what I had. The captain called my mother again. At first she was upset but then settled down, and promised she would call me. She didn't. But on Valentine's Day, I received a sweet letter and pictures. I look like my mom.

I made plans to visit a close friend in Illinois and called an aunt, my birth mother's sister, so that I could meet her. While in Illinois, I visited the Cradle and what used to be the Salvation Army hospital. Then my friend and I drove to Indiana to meet my aunt. When she saw me, she squealed with delight that I looked just like my mother. We went to her room at the motel and she asked me to sit down because she had something to tell me about my father. My friend Anita and I both knew it was not going to be good news.

Until that moment, I thought my mother had become pregnant with me through a love gone wrong but that is not the way it happened. She had been molested by a boarder in her house but she never told her mother because of the fear he instilled in her. So she made up a story about my father and was sent away to have me. After my birth, she went to live with her father. While she was living with her father, this horrid man turned on my mother's two younger sisters. After two years of this, my aunt told a teacher in school. He was arrested and spent 14 years in prison.

I was in shock. I remember thinking to myself: "Goddess, please don't let me deal with this until I get home. Please, I don't want to deal with this right now." I wrote a letter to my birth mother that night, explaining I knew the circumstances of my birth. I told her I realized it would take time before she could see me because old wounds were reopened. I would be patient.

After I got home, I was a basket case. I cried all day, went from window to chair, from chair to window. I didn't know what this revelation meant. Did it make me bad, tainted, what? I cried some more. My daughter called and could tell something was wrong, and when my husband called to tell me he would be late, I broke down and said "No, you have to come home, I am falling apart."

They rushed home. Held me. Cried with me. And assured me I was no different. I calmed down, and when everyone got busy with his or her evening tasks, I went to my altar under a huge poplar tree in the yard, lit my candle, and talked to the Goddess. "Please give me a sign you are here, Hera, Mother of all. I feel alone. I am scared. Please show me you are close and hear my pleas but don't make me look for a sign. I am too tired. I do not have the strength to look." And with that I sat for a while, squeezed the flame out on the candle, and went to bed.

The next morning, looking out the kitchen window across the cornfield, I saw something strange and out of place. I went outside, and coming toward me was the biggest, most beautiful peacock I have ever seen. From out of nowhere came this magnificent fowl with his tail spread wide open, dancing toward me. I sat on the ground and buried my face in my hands and cried for all I was worth.

The Goddess didn't make me look for a sign. She showed up in person. She was near. She heard my call, and felt my empty heart. She had always been there. This was one Mother that had not failed me.

That evening, my husband and two of my daughters were in the barnyard lot watching Hera dance her dance, and I was strutting with her, trying to make the same sounds Hera did. We were dancing together when we noticed a huge white oak snake slith-

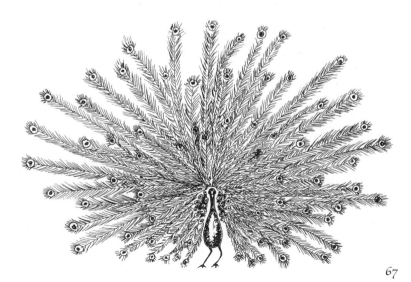

ering through the grass. All of the women took off running and Hera flew up on the barn. When we reached the house, I began to laugh because Kali Ma had dropped in too. My heart mended, and I knew everything would eventually work out fine.

I received another letter from my mother and she referred to herself as my mother, and said she always thought of me on my birthdays and holidays. She named me Laura when I was born and that's the only name she refers to me by. I am her Laura. She thanked me for my patience. We will meet one day when the Goddess thinks we are both ready.

Until that day, I dance my dance to the moon each week, and Hera—well, Hera sits on my roof every night to roost. She won't let anything befall my home.

—*Barbara Harrell*

The moment the consciousness of the Goddess really hit me was in the early 1980s, at a workshop with my teacher, Oh Shinnah. We had experienced a powerful women's ceremony that she conducts and were gathered to process our experiences. I suddenly realized that She had been with me all my life, and that my mother and grandmother knew her too in the person of Mary. I remembered all the ritual acts they did, the prayers, and how Mary's pictures and statues were a constant presence. In that moment, I understood that She was woven underneath and throughout our lives, for generations. A few years after my experience at that workshop, I began teaching a course at our local community college called "Remembering the Feminine" which gave women an experience of the Goddess as part of their lives.

Several years ago, I was initiated in ancient ceremony as a priestess. I'd prepared for this for 12 years. The initiation involved putting my body through a huge fire three times. I learned total trust in Her, faced the possibility of death, and learned to surrender or give myself over totally. In those moments, I and everyone else in the circle was enveloped in Her love. I experienced oneness with everyone and everything around me. The fire spoke to me, as did the trees. Her power was palpable and She was in me and I in Her.

Since that time, I have become more outspoken and public in "standing for" Her. I find myself full of confidence in situations where I'd never speak out formerly such as in my role in the Roman Catholic Church as a cantor, musician, and liturgist.

When I became conscious of Her in my life, it had strong effects. My husband and I separated for three years and I realized that my perception of myself was filtered through him. Those years of raising four children alone while going to nursing school gave me self-confidence and strengthened my inner listening. I think that experiencing the Goddess and Her weaving through us women pushed me into creating a wonderful circle of women for support.

My spiritual practices, my roles, etc. are all deepening and widening as I play out the gifts I've been given. I am called upon to stand for the Goddess (especially in the church) more and more, be it in questions of language or ritual, healing or society. I have little fear around this. In fact, I find myself joyfully getting in confrontational situations, which is a major change for me.

—*Melinda Gardiner*

My realization concerning the Goddess occurred over a period of time. In the 1970s, I became interested in things of the spirit and got involved with Tibetan Buddhism, meditation, and T'ai chi.

During a meditation session, something stuck in my mind and I started to think "that this is not for me. Meditation is a way for men to overcome their egos." At that time, feminism was strong, and assertiveness training was an idea that was catching on. Women were working to feel our power and our strength.

Then I read *The First Sex* by Elizabeth Gould Davis, which is about early cultures and the Great Goddess. I read that all human beings are female until they are washed with a hormone bath in the womb if they're supposed to be male.

With nine other women, I co-founded the Alliance for Women in Architecture in 1972 and then in 1973, helped found the Archive of Women in Architecture, which collected work from 900 American women architects. In architecture, women have something else to offer, a whole different approach to the environment, to ecology, to space, to people, to children, to daily life. We're more realistic, down to Earth, concerned for others, less concerned with building ego monuments to ourselves.

I experimented with open marriage and came to see it as a very Goddess-inspired kind of relationship because I was free. I was like the classic virgins, a woman unto herself, self-creating, not tied to a man . . . even though I was married. I had deliberately chosen a relationship that was committed although not committed exclusively when it came to love and sex and intimacy and soul-sharing.

The Goddess also helped me accept my body as a big woman. I have been inspired by role models who are large and considered powerful in their societies maybe because they are large, like African market women and Polynesian matriarchs and so on. Now I carry myself like a priestess and a Goddess and when I travel people come around and want to take their kids' pictures with me because I'm abundant and they think I'll bring them good health and all good things.

In my professional life, my discovery of the Goddess gave me strength to consciously teach architecture as a woman. Now I teach what I call "oracular architecture," taking students on guided imaginings. I introduce them to the Tarot and talk about oracles and divination and how to contact the collective unconscious, get them to listen to their work, to quiet their egos, to be receptive, and to bring out the yin in themselves.

—*Mimi Lobell*

I don't know that there was ever a time in my life when some kind of loving, guiding, spiritual energy was not present or known. Spirit kept me alive and moving forward during a very grim, repressed childhood in a dysfunctional, claustrophobic family situation.

I was nourished with good reading and directed to sources of information that set me upon a spiritual path that led directly to the work I'm doing now. The sense of being educated and directed by Spirit has never left me and is operative now even though I don't know if I can define all this specifically as Goddess-sent.

I'd say my first official moment of awareness of "The Goddess" came from my readings during the feminist and feminist spirituality movements of the '70s during and after college. My first official involvement was back in the late '80s with a lesbian group that practiced Wicca. Clearly, this concept of "The Goddess" gives back to women an identity and power that had been brutally crushed by patriarchy. It is revolutionary.

In the late eighties, I traveled for the first time in Africa—to Ghana and the Ivory Coast—and thereby touched ancestral land. I learned about the woman warrior Yaa Asantewaa who led the Ashanti in their resistance against the British army. A few years later, I would take her name legally as my last name.

I had my first lesbian experience. I came out and joined the vibrant and diverse queer community of New York. My involvement in spiritual practice and teaching became more public and community oriented, and I began to build a reputation and an acknowledged body of experience. I became involved with a couple of recovery programs for people with dysfunctional family relationships. This marked a major breakthrough. My experience in these recovery programs greatly accelerated my spiritual as well as psychological development. After a few negative experiences with lesbian partners, I met the woman who would become my life partner and we began our life together.

Am I still going through changes? Honey, aren't we all! Now I'm in my late forties, and I love being middle-aged. I will probably adore being old. I love life and learning. It ain't always easy but it is always rewarding. My major change in the past couple of years has been about being able to own my intuitive abilities, nurture them, speak of them openly without euphemism or compromise, utilize them professionally. It is harder to come out this way in this society than it is to come out as queer, and that is plenty hard.

—*Eva Yaa Asantewaa*

Most of my life I had felt a deep pain, a "cultural schizophrenia" that contributed to the disparity I experienced between the world in which I lived and my intuitive sense that there had to be something greater than what I was being told. Not only had I felt the social, political, and emotional gaps in my education and experience, I also felt something was missing in my spiritual environment. My friendships with strong women helped me survive through some pretty bleak years and some of my most influential relationships were with lesbian friends.

I was having trouble with God and the masculinization of the language of the divine when, reading *The Women's Room* by Marilyn French, something clicked. I realized I identified more with the women characters in the book than I did with most of the male characters who peopled my life. This awareness deepened as I read *My Mother, My Self* by Nancy Friday and I was off on a new adventure, discovering the strong feminine within me.

Later I developed a close relationship with a bisexual man in my massage class who was involved with gay and fairy communities. One night when we were camping together, we began talking about contemporary Earth spirituality and paganism. He brought out a book he said had been meaningful in his spiritual development, *The Spiral Dance* by Starhawk. He began reading some passages and my hair stood on end. I heard the names of Goddesses, some of whose names I remembered from Greek and Roman mythology, but here the energy was totally different, something very alive. That night the sky was pulsing with light, the Earth's heartbeat sounded rhythmically in my ears, and my body vibrated with new frequencies. As we slept close together that night, the Goddess held him and me firmly in Her arms and I knew I had been brought face to face with something I longed for.

Following this discovery, I felt confirmed in my sense that men, the patriarchy, had ripped off true spirituality, had raped the Earth, oppressed women and native cultures around the world, and misled and programmed me to believe and live a pack of lies. I looked for every justification I could find to deepen my rejection of the masculine.

I pored through books on women's spirituality, engaged in passionate discussion with women and some men, exploring our spiritual realities and relationships with the Goddess. I experienced myself through much of this time as a lesbian in a male body.

One morning I was standing naked in front of a large mirror in the bathroom, looking at this crazy man, and it hit me, rolled me like a tidal wave. I saw this male body and felt the pain of my revulsion and rejection of the male-in-me. I felt like dying, hopeless in the face of the contradictions I had created. I couldn't be a lesbian and I hated being a man.

I moved shortly thereafter and as I lived in community on a mountain in northern New Mexico, the healing power of Mother Earth helped me transform my pain and conflict. I realized a state of greater harmony as I offered myself in service to all life: the land, the community, and those who came there on retreat. My life continues to be an exploration of being a man creating in new ways and opening to healthy relationships with the Creator of All That Is, including the energies I've known as the Goddess.

—Christopher

While attending the Catholic funeral of a distant relative, I was bored out of my mind, as always, with words that held no meaning for me. As I looked into the sky above the grave, I wondered what a pagan ceremony would be like. I began to ask, "Inanna, cradle him in your arms and carry him out into the universe."

At that instant, a hawk swooped down and circled over the canopy. I could clearly see the delicate pattern of feathers on its wings. It screeched twice very loudly and flew off into the trees. The hair on my arms stood on end. A connection between the request and the Goddess had been made.

When I told my son, he said my prayer had indeed been answered. I lost my son two years later but I was fortunate that he was home with us at the end. My family and I were there, with the help of Hospice, to care for him. As he left us, I kept talking to him, telling him it was okay to let go, to look for the white light. I kept telling him to look for a white bird flying into the universe and to follow it. So many times after that, I would be thinking of him or listening to his favorite music, and a hawk would appear in the sky nearby. It became natural for me to say "Thank you, Inanna."

This association with Her became a focus for my spirituality and my lifelong love of nature. There is a logical rightness to the rhythms of the natural religion.

I've always been different, an "outsider." This bothered me when I was younger but I'm grateful for it now. It has left me free to pursue ideas with a freedom I might not have had if I stayed on the "path of righteousness." I can say these things without fear of burning at the stake as people in other times of history could not.

One problem I've discovered is that people get very defensive about their own beliefs around me. They say things like: "Maybe some people don't believe in Him, but I trust in the Lord" not realizing we are all on the pathways to the same truth. Christ, Allah, Jehovah, Krishna, the Goddess are all names. They are personifications of our goal of oneness with the life-giving force of the universe, the force that holds it all together and makes it work. Somehow, the fact that I follow the "Earth religion" or (oh, breathe it softly!) paganism sets me apart, makes me different. To me, the difference is a matter of blue eyes or brown. Whatever the color, they enable us to see.

—Lucy Harrison

I was on a trip with my husband in my capacity as an anthropology/sociology professor to "measure" the Marian apparitions that had occurred at a site in Medjugorje, a village in the former Yugoslavia. In a very short period of time, I found myself moving from being a participant and observer into a conversion experience. Several paranormal events happened to prime my psyche: winds inside the church, cocks crowing after dark, complete silence of all traffic sounds at the time of the daily apparition. While I did not see this as a "Goddess" figure at that time, it appears likely that the figure has been appearing with more and more frequency as a counterbalance to apocalyptic events such as greed, violence, pollution, etc. Millions of people have recently had these experiences all over the world.

As a result of my experience in Yugoslavia, I became a "pillar of the church," volunteered at a hospital emergency room, and became a parish council member and church lector. I feel I am softer, less hostile, kinder to everyone, have more empathy with my grown-up kids, and am more loving in general. My creative energies have been unlocked. I took up painting.

—*Mary Brenneman*

I should start by saying that because of my life experiences, I don't believe in a divine being that orchestrates things for the good. When I was a little girl, my parents and I managed to escape Nazi Europe. Even though I prayed for them every night, most of our family was murdered during the Holocaust. That was the end of my belief in God. So for me, discovering the Goddess was not a religious experience or even a mystical one, although I've had those. It was, nonetheless, a profoundly empowering and illuminating experience.

Over the past two decades, I have studied dominator and partnership patterns in different cultures. I identified configurations that transcend conventional categories such as right vs left, religious vs secular, capitalism vs communism. Because there were no terms to describe these patterns, I named them the "dominator" and "partnership" models. Central to each of these different patterns is the status of women. I saw that religion reflects and reinforces social structure, and that the return of the Goddess is a major factor in the push toward a partnership society.

I say "return" because although I started my work with contemporary and historical societies, there were prehistorical societies that were oriented more to the partnership rather than the dominator model, societies in which female deities had great power. The work of archaeologists such as Marija Gimbutas, James Mellaart, and Nicolas Platon was very important here, especially that of Gimbutas because she too was interested in the relationship between the Goddess and social structure.

Of course, when I use the term "Goddess" I want to be clear that it's a shorthand. I have no idea whether the prehistorical people who were partnership oriented used such a term. But these people recognized that life comes from the body of woman and that giving and caring for life, rather than taking it, is the most important attribute of the divine.

—*Riane Eisler*

When I was between the ages of 5 and 12, my mother and I attended a fundamentalist Pentecostal Southern Baptist Church. I vividly remember one day in Sunday school (at around 5 years old) when I first heard the story of the Garden of Eden—how Eve ate the apple and was responsible for the suffering of the world. I was shocked but for the first time I understood why my father was so mean, why he beat my mother and punished me so severely. My father was fashioned in the image of God. He could kill us but it would never make up for the sin of being female.

I was a pious child and dutifully took on the responsibility of this Original Sin. Every night I would pray for God to bless everyone in the world. I also prayed to become Eve so that I could save the world. I wouldn't be stupid as to listen to the serpent. Then people would no longer have to suffer.

After graduating from college, I found the work of Joseph Campbell and realized for the first time that the torment I was going through was part of a mythological journey. Instead of going to New York to become a professional dancer, I returned to Mendocino, California, where I had come from, and began to use Campbell's books as an inspiration to explore this revelation through dance.

As it happened, I was given a beautiful studio to live and work in. One night, while studying Campbell's series *The Masks of God,* I read that the biblical tale of the Garden of Eden was a retelling of a much earlier motif in which the garden, the tree, the woman, and the serpent originally represented the deepest spiritual quest. I was utterly stunned. It was suddenly clear that I had not been wrong to pray to become Eve but the Eve I needed to be was not the Christian Eve but the earlier Eve, the Goddess.

I asked myself what ground I was standing on. I saw that I had been cut off at the ankles and my bloody stumps had been planted on the ground of the Punitive Father. At that moment, I devoted my life to finding the sacred ground under my own feet—to rediscover the original woman, the tree, the serpent, the garden, and myself.

Although I became conscious of the idea of the Goddess through the work of Joseph Campbell in 1970, She had been a powerful unnamed presence throughout my childhood on the Mendocino coast of northern California. I grew up wandering, climbing, playing, and dreaming in the undisturbed redwood forest and along the wild and rocky coast. I felt as though someone spoke to me in that whispering cathedral of trees in a voice that only I seemed to hear. (It was years before I realized that the forest did not go on forever and that people were cutting it down, an unthinkable tragedy.)

After I finally could name this presence as Goddess, it was several years before I met anyone who could relate to this concept. *When God Was a Woman* (1976) by Merlin Stone was a great discovery. In 1977 my daughter Sorrel was born at home while we were surrounded by a circle of loving women. We had prepared for her birth for months, rediscovering our own women's rituals of nurturing. It was as though a deep layer of ancient memory was spontaneously rising.

In 1979, I eagerly attended a Goddess conference at the University of California–Santa Cruz and was excited to know there were other women who were tuned to this frequency. Although I have no particular belief in reincarnation, it began to feel more and more as though we were beginning to converge in this life with instruction and wisdom from another time.

In the 1980s, I began attending public lectures by Joseph Campbell, after a decade of absorbing his written work. He often spoke of the archaeologist Marija Gimbutas, acknowledging that her work was a missing link in his own scholarship. My entire system began to ring with his description of her work and I immediately purchased a copy of *Goddesses and Gods of Old Europe*. There She was on every page! I was electrified.

—*Joan Marler*

For me, the Goddess was a process of revelation, an unconscious force that was always with me. I became more clearly conscious of this when I started to make art and write poetry because there was a lot of Goddess imagery coming up and the word "Goddess" kept recurring. When I look back, I realize it has been a thread throughout my life and it seems completely natural to me.

I was really connected to my mother and thought of her as a divine being in our polarized male/female family. I had three older brothers and because of that, I was always aware, in a certain way, of feminist issues. But you can't name those things while you're young. So when I left home for Berkeley and became involved in feminism, these issues just seemed as natural to me as my skin.

I remember one experience that really changed me. I attended a lecture by Marija Gimbutas and heard her say that in the Neolithic era, people had lived in peace. This stunned me because I always felt war and violence were human nature so Marija's words were quite revolutionary to me.

—*Starr Goode*

In 1985, I accepted an invitation to talk about prehistoric symbols at a seminar for historians who studied this era—there were three of us—and Jungian psychologists. I had no idea what to say. The date came closer and closer and at last Minerva, She who is the Warrior and moon, appeared to me and all my thinking changed.

I was very happy when I discovered Marija Gimbutas's *Goddesses and Gods of Old Europe* and her articles in the *Encyclopedia of Religion* because all of a sudden, I knew I was not alone.

Our predecessors considered it wrong to represent divinity only as feminine or masculine. They understood that even though all animals are divided by gender, it is the species and not the gender that counts. Humanity is not female or male but the sum of both.

—*Kristina Berggren*

There was no room for my feminist leanings in the church I attended in Colorado Springs. So I left the church and was in a kind of vacuum. I had found feminism, a spiritual awakening for me, and that had been going on for several years when I came across the work of Elizabeth Gould Davis.

I met Karen Vogel [co-creator, with Vicki, of the *Motherpeace* cards] and together we moved to Berkeley to start writing. She was a feminist anthropologist and I was a feminist historian and our joint project asked what happened to women's power in the past.

Early in 1977, I had what I describe as a kundalini experience, a big stream experience where, in the middle of the night, I awakened in a trance. I couldn't go to sleep. I had started to do yoga so

I was aware that it was a pleasant energy. Then suddenly I felt myself shooting out of the top of my head. It was profound, unbelievable. Everything was black except for stars. As I was dissolving into the night sky, I heard a voice say "I am one with all witches through all time."

Prior to that time, I didn't have any connection with the idea of reincarnation or anything like that. But after that experience of going out of my body and hearing that voice, I felt that that must be true, that I had lived many times before and that I had some connection with witches. I found out later that the night this happened, February 1, is Candlemas, the night of the witches' initiation.

The night I made this connection, Karen and I were in our room together, and she was reading something aloud. I asked her not to continue because I felt something was happening in the room. Then she said to me "Did you feel the room tilt?"

I felt a pressure on my skin, then this tie-dyed wall hanging we had in the room opened up like a round screen and images began to project on it of Amazons and Gorgons and Goddesses. This went on for a while, these images and then words that I could not read. By this time, I felt this incredible love or sacred energy and I was crying. I felt disturbed that I could not read the letters and said that in my mind. They dissolved and reconfigured into English. The whole thing was undulating and moving and the words said "Helena, heal all, hell no" and finally "I am all" over and over again. Then there were these two spiders in an embrace—and that was it.

Ever since then, all the work in my life has come out of that vision. The *Motherpeace* cards were made after that. I began to heal, my headaches went away, my ulcer went into remission, and I was pain-free for the first time. I was healthy.

For a time, Karen and I deliberately stayed out of touch with the news. We felt it was toxic and wanted to have a break from it. We were completely in our own little world, doing our writing and our drawing. Then I got a boil on my back, a really terrible, painful boil. I'd never had anything like it before. We were doing natural things for it and on the sixth day, Karen was putting hot packs on it and I said, "It feels like a volcano that wants to go off." The next day, Mount St. Helens blew and my boil blew.

That brought another level of understanding. It's real. It's physical. I really am part of Her body. Her body is my body. There's no distinction. And I wondered, why am I connected like this?

Since that time, I have done much research on women and the oracular function and I think it's part of our blood mysteries, that we really are mouthpieces, like the Pythia of Delphi. Just as snakes know when an earthquake is going to happen, so do we. In fact, we know a lot of things but we don't have any way of accessing that information because we've shut down those faculties on a conscious level.

In a personal sense, I feel this underlying structure of the Goddess is alive and intelligent and loves me. I always think of it as Mother and I always have, since the very first contact.

No matter what happens to me, I feel faith because I know I am in good hands.

—Vicki Noble

I would say I gradually became aware of the Goddess over a period of several years, and that the Goddess affirmed a personal value system I have had from childhood. Perhaps the closest event to a "moment" of discovering the Goddess was seeing Dr. Marija Gimbutas's book, *The Language of the Goddess,* in a bookstore and buying it because of the symbols and images in the book. It was an "Aha! So that's what these symbols and images mean" moment.

The consequences were clarity and a greater commitment to engendering the personal values of honoring and nurturing life, and working toward social change. I regained clarity about my life, that it is on the right track, and that I must stay committed to my personal values. It also gave me a sense of commitment toward my community that I had previously lacked.

The Goddess and the consequences of cultural transformation inherent in Neolithic Goddess civilizations taught me how to work toward change, and what that change would look like. Specifically, I wrote an article on social change on a macro-level, on how to change from a dominator society to a cooperative, mutually beneficial society. I wrote three new myths for children of the 21st century based on Goddess civilization values as a way to help nudge us toward a post-patriarchal society based on life-honoring values.

On a deeply personal level, my connection with the Goddess gave me back a core set of values that had become muddied by patriarchy. These values have been renewed and are stronger now, with a clarity I had lost in my adult years. It renewed my sense of wisdom.

I am still going through changes. Essentially, however, the core remains clear and strong to guide me. I discovered the Goddess during my transition from being an emotionally dependent person to being an emotionally independent one. Now I am trying to make the transition from independence to interdependence.

—*Imogene Drummond*

I grew up in a quiet town in the far south of New Zealand in the midst of a large, loving, extended family and the strong bonds of the local community. The town is off the main road in a fertile valley, surrounded by rolling green hills. As a child, I often came home from school, put on my gumboots, and went walking by myself in the gentle folds of those hills.

It was a good beginning but my adolescence was difficult. The culture I was immersed in was characterized by deep political conservatism and the moral strictures of Presbyterian fundamentalism where there was no welcome for my sexual emergence. My parents were dismayed by the abundance of my energy and my insatiable challenges, questions, and longings for a wider world. I hurt them badly when I declared my loss of faith in their God but I was unable to reconcile the harshness of the Biblical God with either the intense love and beauty of the *Song of Songs* or with my own emerging womanhood.

From very early childhood until I was a young woman, just before sleep or when I woke in the night, I would often enter a state of complete bliss. I felt myself pressing into someone who held me softly and with complete love. The presence was enormously large—perhaps as big as the universe—and comforting, like the soft flesh of a mother. It made me feel very special. The conscious ecstasy would last only an instant because as soon as I realized I was in it, it would go, leaving me still feeling held and connected but not quite inside the wonderful presence.

When I left home, I wrote to my mother about how much I missed the round bosoms and buttocks of the land. The country-side was like the full body of a great, beautiful woman, I said. She remembered that description and occasionally reminded me of it as though she also knew the pull of that feminine power. Neither of us had the language—or heretical audacity, perhaps—to name this as an experience of the Goddess.

A beautiful dancing god sometimes came to me in dreams from adolescence until after I had my first baby. My body would fill with light, and when he invited me to dance and make love I felt my mortality slip away. In my meetings with him, I felt myself become a counterpart to his divinity. The dancing god evoked a consciousness of my own feminine power which had no social mirror.

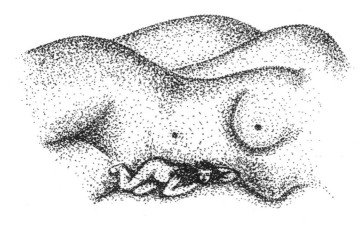

Experiences related to these also came with pregnancy and motherhood. I loved the process of my body softening and rounding as babies grew inside me, and had many ecstatic night feeds with my first baby boy in which I would sometimes feel myself not only holding him but also being held again by the great warm presence of childhood nights.

—*Glenda Cloughley*

My exploration of the Female Divine has been going on since birth. I distinctly remember when I woke up to the idea of healing through creative expression. It was the summer I turned 16 and my Sicilian father took all of us (my mother, sisters 18 and 12, and my 6-year old brother) to Italy for the summer. I was in San Marco, in Venice, at vespers listening to the monks chant and I began to cry. Late that night, I awoke to the full moon flowing over the velvet sea and illuminating me, and I knew I would become an artist healer.

Ministers make my skin crawl and I am suspicious of women in the clergy. I do, however, love to visit churches in Europe, light candles, sing (as in Matisse's chapel in Vence, France), walk the labyrinth in Grace Cathedral in San Francisco, and meditate in Buddhist, Taoist, and Hindu temples.

When I moved to Japan in 1979, I had extraordinary experiences in the temples. One time I merged with the Goddess of Mercy's statue. Later, while paying homage to the Paper Goddess high in the mountains in Her shrine, She gave me a vision of Her snowing paper all over the Earth to heal our hearts. After this, I began a series of works with paper and dance, my "Canto" series.

While living in Hong Kong, I had an intense dream that my name was changed to "lion."

About nine months after my husband John's death from Lou Gehrig's disease, I returned to our sacred secret camping spot in Big Sur, our source of inspiration and where we wed. I had been afraid to go there, afraid of the depths of my despair, and indeed one afternoon I passed out on the shore from the intensity of my keening.

My third night there, the winds came up, waves were pounding on the shore, the bushes were rustling, and the spirits were about. I made my campfire strong and began to gong my Tibetan singing bowl close to my ear to disassociate my conceptual mind. Slowly, I broke my internal silence. "I'm afraid," I spoke into the bowl and struck it. "I'm afraid to speak. I'm afraid to dance. I'm afraid to paint. I'm afraid to perform. I'm afraid to write." After each utterance, I gonged the bowl. Late into the night, it rained slightly and in the morning, a storm was hovering and I knew it was time to leave. Walking across the two miles of beach to the path carrying my belongings, remembering the past night, I realized "I'm afraid of everything I love." Hissing cat growl. Right there by my ankle was a bobcat! Green metallic eyes and mine locked. The bobcat was telling me to take notice.

The second time I saw a big cat, I was in Jerusalem for an arts festival. Still grieving for my husband, I went walking in the Ein Gheddi Reserve above the Dead Sea. Climbing, climbing in the morning heat, a MIG jet overhead interrupting my solitude, I came to a stream that went through a reed tunnel. I began to crawl, stopped to loosen my neckerchief, to soak it in the cool water, and squeeze it on my head and neck. Crawling out into the light, my eyes went up a paw and into the eyes of a leopard! I yelled so loud, the sandstone cliffs reverberated and paralyzed us. Green metallic eyes and mine were riveted to one another. Slowly, almost imperceptibly, the leopard began to gingerly walk down the side of the mountain.

I had two more encounters with large cats, one in Northern California with a puma and another when a car I was in passed a truck from which I could see a tiger's tail swinging out of the window while the big cat nuzzled the driver, having a grand time.

When I saw the Çatal Hüyük Magna Dea seated on her lion's throne, I made the connection.

—Diana Marto

My first experience of the Goddess was during the natural home birth of my second son in Bristol, England. This was my first realization of my physical and spiritual power. "The Mother" who I saw was a great mass of alternating darkness and light. Stunning.

I came across *The White Goddess* by Robert Graves a few years later and this changed my life forever, setting me on a lifelong search to understand the ancient religion.

My second experience with the Goddess happened on a trip to the ancient Neolithic sites of Avebury, Silbury Hill (Earth's pregnant womb), and West Kennet Long Barrow in south England. I was on a sacred mushroom trip and had an intense experience of the sacred Earth as the Mother who is grieving and in great pain. This changed my life. I went to live in the Welsh countryside to be close to Her and Her seasons.

These experiences of the ancient Mother in the land, in the stones, and in holy wells inspired my paintings for many years. I believe the ancestors and nature spirits—the voices of Earth— speak to us at the sacred sites, and we must learn again to listen. Since the end of the 1960s, I've experienced ancient women, sisterhoods which exist in other realms or co-exist with us in a continuum of past, present, and future. These have been communicated to me in visions and dreams and this ancient source has inspired my paintings.

—*Monica Sjöö*

I would identify myself from very early on as a spiritual person, someone who was seeking, having dreams, trying to understand the mysteries, spending a lot of time in nature, pondering. Even as a small child I remember this. But so much depends on what's available for understanding and in my family and culture there was nothing but Christianity. I remember finding this tiny little book on Zen on a bookshelf in our library, and I just pored over that little book.

I remember a dream I had in which an old woman who used to take care of me brings me a box which she says contains my treasure. Inside, there's a perfect white round stone. Suddenly in my journal there's just this one phrase "eleven thousand Paleolithic sketches of women dancing found near Cologne."

In college, I started studying philosophy, anthropology, existentialism, different spiritual traditions, and a deeper level of Christianity. I felt I was pressing, pressing, pressing right up against the big questions: What is it? Who am I? What is this all about? What is the right path through this crazy world?

All of this was incremental, incremental, and then boom—the Goddess came in, and it really felt like ground to stand on. Suddenly my seeking was over. Now I know there is no final answer, there is no final way, there is no final anything. It's just an ever-expanding universe.

When I came upon the Goddess in my late twenties, I became a part of a movement that was just being born. [Catherine began doing photography and exhibiting her work. She also became politically active.] I turned my life over to the Goddess in a certain way, and I'm always asking "Goddess guide me, Goddess guide me. Stay inside me. Goddess guide me."

When you start doing that, life changes.

—*Catherine Allport*

My first initiation to the archetypal Goddess was before I even knew anything like that existed. I was eleven years old and to me "woman" was my mother, a distant, punitive authority, and my grandmothers who were loving and indulgent but who had no power next to my mother. It was from them that I got the affection I craved.

I lived in the hills of northern New Jersey in 1961, a place where George Washington slept during the American Revolution and whose farms boasted Jersey corn, tomatoes, and Guernsey milk. The winters were cold and snowy. We lived at the end of a winding road and I had to walk about one-quarter mile through a lightly wooded area to the highway to be picked up by the school bus. One day in the middle of a snowstorm, my mother insisted that I wear leggings—a pair of corduroy pants—to school under my dress to keep warm. I despised those leggings, a badge of childhood in a school where girls with big hairdos rode to school on the backs of motorcycles. I felt out of place and ridiculed as a child. I wanted to be grown up.

So I quickly donned my coat and scurried out the door before my mother could inspect my outfit, quite pleased with myself for getting away with not wearing the dreaded leggings. I walked a treacherous path that early morning. The road was slick with a thick layer of ice, making it difficult to walk on the steep hills without falling. While I usually met some neighbors walking to the bus, this morning I was alone.

I stood on the corner at the edge of the woods, looking at the deserted highway. Barely a car passed and it was very quiet. It began to snow, slowly at first, then heavily. I became cold since I was standing still. As time progressed, I wondered where the other children were. It was so quiet. I couldn't go home since I would be in trouble and probably reprimanded for not wearing my leggings.

I believe I stood there in the snowstorm for two hours. As it became lighter and the snow stopped falling, I realized the bus was not coming that day. Numb from the waist down and in both arms, I slowly struggled up the road. It was dead quiet. As I turned to go up the steep, icy hill, I was overcome with the impulse to sleep. "I will just lie down here for a moment," I thought, "then I will have the energy to get up the hill." I lay down in a soft snow drift and instantly fell asleep.

I was immediately dreaming and that dream is as vivid today, forty years later, as it was then. I was swimming down, very deep, under the sea. There were different colored fish, all smiling, and people. As I reached the sea floor, there was a lady sitting there. She was very large, oversized. She sat on a throne yet gave the impression of moving and swaying rather than sitting still. She reached out for me and sat me on her lap. I looked up into her face. It was very beautiful and she was dressed in clothes like purple velvet and had a crown on her head. I was not afraid. On the contrary, I was completely happy, content, and safe.

She smiled at me. "Oh no," she said softly. "It is not your time yet. You have much yet to do in your life." I wanted to stay with her but she began swimming up to the surface, carrying me in her arms. As we reached the surface, I came awake, jolted by the muted sounds of children crying out in play. I was instantly self-conscious. "I must get up and walk," I said to myself, "or the children will find me and make fun of me sleeping here in the snow."

It was a long, slow struggle to move and walk home. When I knocked on the door and my mother saw me, she was furious. I was covered in ice and very cold. I took off my wet clothes, she being angry all the while, and crawled into bed. The process of thawing out was painful. I cried for help. My mother told me it was my punishment for disobeying her. I lay there all day. When my father came home and saw me lying in the bed, there was a huge fight between them, as he felt I had not been cared for properly. I am still moved by that memory of him fighting my cause.

Over the years, I have never forgotten "the lady." I have never seen Her again, but I have no doubt that I will when I pass over to the other side. I often ponder Her words during times of trouble and traumatic change. I feel I was meant to do what I do now and look for meaning in a larger framework than just my own life.

In the early 1980s, I was at a slide show given by a tarot reader, Susan Levitt. She had journeyed to Europe to record Goddess sites. At the beginning of the show, she instructed us to look for images that were familiar. Toward the end of the show, I saw the Lady of my dream. It was Juno Regina in divine splendor upon Her throne with Her crown and scepter. It was the first time I had seen an image of Her. She is very proud. She is the ruler of femininity and directly in line with other Goddesses like Isis (our Lady of bread), and Cybele, the mountain Mother worshipped as a black stone. Goddesses encompass all stages of life, activities, and passages in my womanness. I had never seen a Goddess image before I saw my Lady's crown and blue mantle when I was a child. I have often wondered where that image came from. If there is an internal knowledge of the Goddess that is passed through women, the Queen of Heaven lives within me.

Since that lecture, I have adopted the imagery of a Juno spirit as part of the inner force that makes me female. I meditate on this before sleep and ask for guidance. I let Her be the guide through my menstrual period, a time that is often a mass of emotional and physical ailments, especially now with the onset of menopause. During those times, I let go of rational thought and allow myself to be linked to all women, past and present. I found a reference saying that Juno did some work under the sea, but it is not commonly known. I prefer to think of Her there. This image inspires me with hope and trust in the renewal of life.

—*Beth Hensperger*

I had this dream: I am in an old house. A door opens and an old, old woman wearing a long dress comes out of the door carrying an armful of golden wheat. It is a gift for me. She sprinkles it in front of me—very ritualistically—making sure it forms a beautiful mound. I marvel at the beauty of the wheat and the perfect mound it makes. Then the old woman says, "Follow me." She turns and walks back through the door and begins to slowly climb a long, long flight of stairs. I follow her to the door. I watch her climb into the darkness. I want to follow but my brain won't let me. It insists that I wake up.

I work on my dreams with Patricia Reis once a month. Once, while typing out my dreams in preparation for a session with her, I almost fell off my chair. I rushed downstairs to my work space to look at a little woman I had created from a leftover piece of clay a week before. Here was the woman from my dream—the Great Mother. It was a stunning experience.

—*Patricia Hubbard*

I remember at a young age drawing a picture of a man with many eyes and a woman with many arms. My parents pointed to the man, asking: Who is this? That's God, I explained. He needs lots of eyes so He can see everything. They pointed to the woman, and asked: And who's she? That's Mrs. God. She needs lots of hands so She can help people and take care of things. My parents thought I was a strange and precocious boy-child, but it's obvious that even at age five, I knew.

I've had two peak experiences concerning the Goddess. First, while attempting to scout an appropriate location on Mosholu Parkway in New York to celebrate the Wiccan Sabbat Beltane in 1974, I injured my foot. Wrapping the foot in an Ace bandage, I led the ritual the next day with the limping step of the goat-foot god. To assuage the pain, I began chanting the Green Tara mantra every morning and evening. For several months, this enabled me to walk on a painfully swollen foot. Six months after the injury, I awoke with pain in the foot, got a friend to drive me to the hospital, and was told the X-rays showed that I had broken the foot half a year earlier but it had healed with no complications. The doctor couldn't understand why I had the pain but I assumed it was because Green Tara wanted me to know She had completed the healing. The break never bothered me again.

The second experience occurred while I was living in Flushing in 1980. I had discovered a beautiful Hindu temple on Bowne Street and began to go there at least twice a month to make offerings to the deities and enjoy its peaceful ambiance. One Navaratri (the nine-night autumn festival honoring Durga, virgin warrior Goddess of the pantheon) I knelt before Her altar and suddenly became aware that each of the many altars to the Gods and Goddesses had images of their animal vehicles set before them. A rat bowed before Ganesha, a bull knelt before Shiva, and so on. But the image of Durga was situated where a vehicle statue would obstruct traffic so She did not have Her lion before Her. However, I was kneeling before her and my given name is Leonard which means "like a lion." A chill went up my spine, the hairs on the back of my neck stood up, and I felt the palpable presence of the Goddess before, above, and within me, as I assumed the lion pose of Hatha yoga and said "Jai, Durga Ma—I am your vehicle."

At that time, I had been having a series of repeating dreams, nightmares in which I suddenly came upon a lion and fled as it pursued me. Once I decided to take on the role of the Goddess's lion, the nightmares stopped.

—*Len Rosenberg*

I think I have known of the Goddess since I was a small child in Sweden. I always felt I had to follow my own nature, not what I was told and I did know there was something more, larger, though I did not know how to name it. In my teens, I was a part of many worlds because we moved and I was always having to make new friends but then was not able to keep in contact since we were living in different parts of the world. I was also very unhappy at the dissolution of my family.

Then I read *The Once and Future Goddess* by Elinor Gadon and other texts, and there was a recognition. Then the Goddess appeared to me in my paintings as "eternal woman."

As a result of this experience, my life has changed. I am showing my work primarily with women and am not competing in the New York art scene. I think that, in some ways, this helps my work speak to women.

I also hope, in the future, to live a simpler life, in the country, with the stars and the seasons, growing in a spiritual practice that is balanced with reading and painting and some friends sometimes, with my husband and son not too far away.

Currently I am waiting for the clarity or knowledge I need to follow my intuitive self, which has always been what guides my life. Meanwhile, I am "hanging," having many experiences of self-doubt over what I should do, how, where, when. But I know this is a part of my journey, that I will be stronger, and all will be clear at some point.

—*Agathe Bennich*

I became intellectually aware of the Goddess in the women's movement in the 1970s. I was looking at the Goddess as an archetype of women's power and empowerment—power in ancient times and empowerment in today's society.

My relationship to the Goddess grew beyond the intellectual when I had my first Goddess experience. It was in the middle of the night while I was on a trip to Greece. I saw an apparition of light, a kind of blue light that came through the door when I was asleep. In fact, my cat was very aware of it and started crying. A few hours later, the phone rang and a friend in New York said that my partner, Gail, was having "visions of the Goddess" and was in quite a state. I broke my trip and returned to New York to find Gail in the midst of a powerful spiritual experience. My parallel experience in Greece was clearly a summons from the Goddess to help Gail through this episode. This fact broke my "intellectual-only" relationship to the Goddess and pierced me to my very soul.

After these experiences, my attitude about the Goddess changed to an ardent religious kind of state, one that reinforced everything I believed about the essence of the women's movement. I suddenly saw the meaning of the art and mythology I had been raised with in Athens, Greece—the home of Athena, the home of the Goddess.

I started writing about the Goddess in feminist magazines I helped publish in New York and Greece. I participated in Goddess groups.

In the 1980s, I had a bout with cancer. After it was over, Gail and I went to a Goddess conference in Crete, and attended an intense all-night worship. By dawn, I was in a visionary state. I walked out of this beautiful hotel by the sea. The beach was deserted and the sun had not come up yet. I walked down to the water and sat and looked at it. I felt I was Persephone mourning for her mother (my own mother had died of cancer a few years before and I had never mourned her). I walked through the darkness into the sunrise and I felt at that moment that I was reborn, healed, and nothing would ever happen to me again.

Since then, I have viewed the Goddess as the Mother Healer of us all. She is the inspiration for my gardens, and the guide leading me to explore and practice various healing arts. In healing others, we heal ourselves. And in healing the earth, we reclaim the female energy which we need in order to balance what has gone on for millennia before us. Like Persephone, we are resurfacing, we are reborn, we are becoming whole.

—*Charoula Dontopoulos*

My dog was with me and sat very quietly, almost as though she was pointing at something, totally rapt. Then I heard laughter coming from something like a blue veil. Then it became like the Blue Fairy in *Pinocchio*. She was huge, She was tall, as tall as a willow tree. She was a big presence and she told me that I could be anything I want. That it was up to me. [Gail later discovers that her partner Charoula, who was in Greece, had a similar vision at the same time.]

My second experience happened on a trip home to visit my parents in Ohio. I walked out into a field at dusk in some despair because the corn is now so uniform. It's genetically engineered and I wondered where the natural part had gone. All of a sudden, I felt this stirring, this sound. I felt that each corn plant could breathe and bend over and that it was animated, that each one was alive in her own unique way and very female. They're all very female. I experienced the Goddess in a cornfield. It seemed each plant was a presence, a whispering part of Her, like a legion of floral Goddesses.

I returned to Ohio after that and became an organic farmer. The Goddess has changed entirely now that I live on the land. She is not outside me. It's as thought I live in Her. Probably every day I catch my breath and feel Her near. I see signs of Her, like a white pigeon among gray ones.

The soil absolutely fascinates me, what it's made up of. The more it dies, the more life comes out of it. I spend a lot of time now in the forest. If we hadn't forgotten about Her, the Earth would be covered with forest and that is where She really is.

—Gail Dunlap

I was on a vision quest in Death Valley, California, with a group led by Adele Getty. I was encamped on the middle of three stair-step mesas, quite high up, overlooking a vast distance across a valley. One day while working in my circle, I looked across the valley to where a line of far-off mountains sank into a kind of V-shaped cleft. There was another, even farther line of far-off mountains, gray in the distance, hundreds of miles away, in this V-shape. It occurred to me that it rather looked like pussy-hair between a women's thighs.

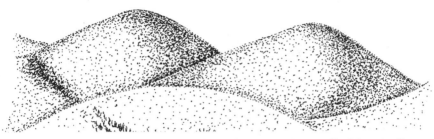

An interesting concept, I thought. My primary Goddess is Ge, oldest of the Greek goddesses, the Goddess who is the Earth (our words ge-ology and ge-ography use Her name) and I believe the Earth is a woman/Goddess. From the cleft, I swept my gaze across the valley, closer to my own position, and then saw a road slicing across the desert sand at an angle. Aha! a scar from a C-section, I smiled. I wondered how far I could carry this analogy.

Bringing my gaze closer to the base of my mesa, I saw (believe this or not) two small round hills—one with a nipple atop it. As I tracked the remaining distance across the sand to the foot of my mesa and then up it and over the edge to where I was standing and up my feet and body, I realized that I was the head and eyes and hands and feet of the Goddess. I am Ge. Ge is me.

There is no question that this realization changed my life on a cellular level. Ge and I had been on a fairly intimate level from the time I was eight, but now it was clear that I was to do Her work in the world—that She acts through me and I act for Her.

I had been active in a Berkeley drumming group—the Emerald Earth Laughing and Drumming Society. We met every week and laughed and cried and sang and drummed and put on large public rituals. Many people brought songs to the group which we learned by ear and sang on a regular basis. At some point, I joined a women's circle and one month our group met with two others for a "chant jam" and I discovered that some songs had many variations. I began wondering why someone didn't contact the authors to find the correct way to sing each song in order to collect them and put them in a book. I waited around for someone to do this, and regularly checked bookstores to see if someone had. Then one day I awoke with the Goddess whispering in my ear that I was the "someone" with the skills to do this.

So I tracked down authors and put together a little chant book called *The Green Earth Spirituality Songbook* and it sold several hundred copies over the years and almost immediately I realized that people were going to keep writing songs and I was going to keep collecting them and that this was going to go on and on, probably for the rest of my life. And one day, a year or so after the chant book was out, I awoke with the Goddess whispering in my ear that She would like another book, a larger book, with several hundred songs in it, and that I was the one to do it.

"No," I said, "but thank you very much for thinking of me. That's going to take a long time, years in fact, and there are several other things I've got in mind for my life."

Over the next year or so, She kept pestering me, becoming more and more demanding. One day I had it out with Her. "No!" I screamed, "I simply won't do this! You're asking too much! This is a five-year project and I don't have five years to give it! Go find someone else to do it for you!"

She was quiet for a few seconds, then whispered calmly "Some day you are going to die and you will come face to face with Me. At that point you are going to have to explain to Me why you did not complete the one task I've given you. I've only asked you to do one thing for Me, and this is it."

And then She left me alone.

So here I am, after seven years of work, having gone through three publishers and many thousands of dollars, having finally decided that what I want to be when I grow up is a book publisher. My company is called Emerald Earth Publishing and *Songs for Earthlings* (all 3,000 copies) arrived on Beltane 1998. It has 433 songs, hymns, chants, and rounds celebrating Earth and all of us who live here. I know She's proud of me and it, and I just wish She'd stop poking me in the middle of the night to give me more ideas on how to market it.

A few years ago, I decided I wanted to find my partner, my real partner, my soulmate. I went through several months of "getting ready." About the middle of April, I felt it was time.

I did ritual without ceasing. On a windy day, I'd ask the wind, who traveled all over the planet, to tell my partner that I was ready and looking for him. I spoke to rushing streams and rivers and called to the ocean. I started a 9-month chakra class and each time we finished a chakra, we did a ritual involving it, and I used the energy of the class to put out a call/prayer for my partner. Then I'd go home and pray at my altar—which I'd set up for the whole nine months. I'd add an object and a corresponding color candle for each chakra.

My women's circle met at my place every week, and I used our energy to ask the Goddess's help on this quest. The circle followed me on my ups ("I think I've found him!") and downs ("Oops, no, he wasn't the right one after all").

In the fall, I did the Church of All Worlds version of the

Eleusinian Mysteries and used that experience too. And at Spring Equinox, when we had the concluding weekend up at Anywfn, I was feeling like, well, maybe this isn't going to work. That night we had a huge bonfire, and I prayed to the fire to help me find my partner.

The following week I decided it would be fine if I didn't find my partner because I had many men around who loved me and their male energy would give me much of what I needed. The week after that I got a message from my brother that my college sweetheart was looking for me—did I want to be found? "Ooooo," my heart sang.

Well, we wrote for several months, then talked on the phone for several more, and before I ever laid eyes on him again I was back in love with him. Eventually I moved to Philadelphia where he was, and we got married.

—Julie Forest Middleton

I first went to Crete in 1978 and was completely overwhelmed by the aspect of the Goddess which permeates that place. Her bare breasted abundance was so common, so dominant at that time in Crete and there was such an acceptance of sensuality, I lactated. So I became one with the feeling of the island.

I think what happened in my personal life is that I became much more accepting of the fullness of my being.

—Hera

My serpentine path to the Goddess began in earnest when my analyst suggested that I read about Aphrodite so that I might evoke more of her archetypal energy into my life. That suggestion led me to Carol Christ's book, *The Laughter of Aphrodite*. Deeply touched by the book, though not knowing exactly why, I wrote and asked Ms. Christ what else she had written, what else she was doing. "Leading pilgrimages to Crete" was the answer.

I was totally unprepared for the tremendous impact that trip was to have on me. It changed my spiritual life—my whole life—profoundly.

I had been to the archaeological museum in Heraklion many times, and Knossos twice but I experienced them in totally new ways this time. It was wonderful.

Carol took us around the museum and showed us the language of the Goddess in the artifacts. It was astounding. I had only viewed them through the eyes of male-oriented archaeology before. Goddess, what a difference!

I probably don't even need to say that Knossos now appeared to me in a totally new way also. Rather than a palace complex ruled by kings, it became a community center where women led people in the worship of the Goddess. It is so lovely, empowering, invigorating to feel the power of the Goddess as it must have felt in the ancient world. And you still feel Her even though Her power is not so evident today.

For three days we used the village of Zaros as our base, a lovely little place in the Psiloritis Mountains. En route to Zaros, we visited the Paliani Convent with its sacred two thousand-year-old myrtle tree and icon of the Virgin Mary. The place had the most incredible effect upon me. I started crying the moment we arrived and didn't stop until we left. Paliani is a convent with all elderly nuns. It has a courtyard with the myrtle tree and icon in it, flowers everywhere, and a church next to the tree and courtyard. People come to Paliani from all over Greece to ask to be healed or to have a wish granted. I wanted to stay forever. We did a lovely ritual there which involved the singing of some sacred songs and the making of a wish. Each of us made a wish or asked for a request to be granted as we tied a ribbon Carol had given us onto the myrtle tree. Everyone was very emotional.

From there, we visited Phaistos and Hagia Triada where we performed a ritual in the oldest part of the site. From Phaistos, we continued to Kalamakia, a lovely, unspoiled, uncrowded beach for food, rest, and a swim. After eating and resting, I walked along the stony beach. It was a bright, warm day. Children and adults frolicked in the water. Some lay on the sand sunning themselves. I had my eyes on the stones. Suddenly I felt connected through the soles of my feet to Mother Earth. It felt so strong, I was shocked. When I looked down at the ground, my eye fell on a green stone shaped like a heart. I thought of Susan Griffin's words: "Behind naming, beneath words, there is something else, Named, Unnamed, Unnameable."

We hiked in the Zagros gorge and visited Archanes, the Minoan sanctuary. High on a mountain peak (with an incredible view of the surrounding countryside) we sang, made music, let go of something (a fear, a loss, whatever) by throwing an offering down a crevice in the mountain just as people had done thousands of years ago.

The presence of our male bus driver,

Yannis, bothered me here. He was the only male and the only out-side observer of our rituals. I felt very inhibited. I was going to talk to Carol about it and ask that he not be allowed to join us later in the day at the Skoteino cave but I changed my mind. As it turned out, Yannis was a great help in the cave and he participated in a rit-ual with a great deal of feeling. He obviously was glad to be part of it all and took it very seriously, not mocking us as I thought he would. And as Carol said later, we need to include male energy, not exclude it.

I now have a very different experience of the divine. Now, when I think of the divine, I feel a strong, almost physical presence of the female Divine. And now I can truly say that I feel that death is followed by rebirth in this wonderful cycle. Before my trip to Crete, I believed this intellectually (or at least tried to) but I did not feel it.

—Joan Cichon

My moment of discovering the Goddess came at a time when I was divorced, my children had left home, and I was wandering about looking for a place to settle down. I had tried to fill my emptiness with jobs, education, and romance but nothing worked. Or as Quakers would say, "A way did not open."

In the late 1970s, someone loaned me a book on Judy Chicago's "Dinner Party." In it there is a section on Goddesses. I picked it up after I had gone into bed and began to read that sec-tion. Prickles went up my the back of my neck. When I finished reading, I turned out the light and slept more deeply than I ever remembered.

The next book I remember reading on the subject was Naomi Goldenberg's *The Changing of the Gods*. Then, one after another, the books that were out at that time just fell into my hands.

At a local Jungian study group, we focused on the story of the Grail for a year. One of the leaders said that the Grail was a symbol of woman, "a cup, empty and passive and waiting for the phallus." This did not jibe with my having been filled with four children and my curious, assertive nature. By that time in my life, I could do without the phallus.

This led me to wonder what was the symbol for woman. I began tearing pages out of magazines, searched greeting card racks, and dug into art history but I found nothing that wasn't from a male point of view. That's how I discovered how pervasive the male point of view was. For ten years, I refused to read anything by a man in an attempt to discover how women think and respond to the world. I put the images I collected in a brown manila envelope that I occasionally lost.

Eventually, I learned how to use a camera and made slides of the pictures I had found. Any place I could find an audience, I showed these slides, asking the women who came to tell me whether they saw themselves or male interpretations of themselves. I listened, I learned, found more imagery, read in libraries, and changed the composition of the slide lectures.

In 1990, a Quaker woman videotaped my slide lectures and we formed a small company called Quaker Video to distribute tapes about Quakers, women, and women's spirituality. Now I did not have to carry a slide projector and screen everywhere.

The changes in my life have been radical. I have been more alone as well as closer to others and almost all of life's other pendulums have begun to swing much more widely. Having gone through such extreme poverty that I was sure I would become a bag lady, I now have confidence that I will be taken care of if I set my priorities right. I serve the Goddess and that is my ministry.

This summer, I am moving into a Quaker community of people who are not yet ready to go into a "Life Care" situation. The outward aspects of my ministry have diminished but there are inward projects which need to be done, genealogy, autobiography, and a general winding up of public affairs. I look forward to this lighter approach to life.

—*Mary R. Hopkins*

As a child I experienced intense mind expansion and an imperative to do work to fulfill this connection, but did not know what it was. As I have grown, I have fused this imperative with my creativity and the journeys I take and now hold it as my life's mission to do the work of that force. I am comfortable now to call the Goddess "energy of the planet, the life force."

Integrating spirituality with conscious intent, existential landscape, and skills is a lifelong journey that takes time and the ability to change. In the last decade, the urgency of this work has intensified, and now I vividly see the Goddess-spirit in a great resurgence as new ways of living burst through the facades of a crumbling patriarchy. I don't know what the new forms are for me yet but I am being asked to clear out old junk, to empty out, to prepare for restructuring. No longer is this focused only on what

I make but on who I am, body as well as spirit, as though the change and creativity is cellular, as though Goddess-spirit is coming directly into my body now. I have been present with enormous female earth energy in my meditations, including huge Goddess-type forms, great-in-scale breathing body forms, very much the Mother Goddess Herself, at the outer edge of my ability to focus on seeing.

—*Suzanne Bellamy*

I was evacuated from London during the blitzes of World War II to a remote village in the Mendip Hills. While living there, I became aware of another form of . . . well, I couldn't define it at the age of eight. But it was a way of life that embraced the Earth as the Mother, that celebrated the seasons and the wheel of the year with simple ceremony and song and dance and magic. I didn't recognize it for what it was until some thirty years later.

My mother, on her frequent visits, seemed at home with this and also with the people. She was an herb woman, as were her mother and her grandmother. It was a magic interlude up among Celtic barrows that ended all too abruptly when my father was moved to the Midlands, we were able to live together again, and it was back to those dreadful nuns and Christianity.

I always remembered the Earth as Mother from this childhood evacuation experience, which was very comforting, and I turned to this memory more and more as I struggled to remain a Christian believer. During the 1970s and early '80s, when I became an ardent feminist and was coming to terms with my long-repressed sexual orientation, the church became less and less relevant to my life.

I loved singing in the prestigious cathedral choir and I loved the liturgy but I tried to tune out the sermons, some of which were futile attempts to rationalize the angry, vengeful, destructive father-God pictured in the Old Testament. Even though I was terrified to look, I was beginning to realize that Christianity was a takeover, a remodeling and reworking, a masculinization and finally repression of the great sacred myths of ancient Goddess worship. I also realized it was a religion that kept its followers in line through fear—fear that they would not earn a place in heaven. Consequently, these followers fear living this life to its fullest.

One of my daughters introduced me to the Feminist Spiritual Community (FSC) of Portland, Maine. I went with dread and fascination to what I feared would be a hotbed of witchcraft and lesbianism. It was, and still is, but it is much, much more. It is a nonjudgmental place of safety for women, a place where whatever you believe, whatever your sexual orientation, you are welcome. It is a place to explore spirituality through ritual, song, meditation, and discussion, to learn how to resolve deep differences, beliefs, and disagreements peacefully and harmoniously.

Through the FSC, I found the Goddess and left the church. I was encouraged and supported in my exploration of my sexuality and in my decision to go back to school. I was honored in a croning ceremony instead of being reviled and ignored for my advancing age. In short, I was accepted as a whole person by the Goddess, just as I was, and as I would become.

I regard my discovery of the Goddess as a speeding up of the change in direction that I was heading toward most of my life. It is difficult to separate the changes that took place when I acknowledged, accepted, and began to live with my sexual orientation from the changes that took place when I rejected Christianity, accepted, and started to live with my spiritual orientation. I had enrolled in theology school in a last-ditch effort to make sense of Christianity, and was active in a drive to rebuild a portion of the cathedral when I left, very abruptly, in a sudden realization that I had lost my faith a long time ago.

The Goddess called to me so strongly that I kept seeing Her in a lovely, carved wooden statue and pictures of the Virgin in the cathedral. I meditated on Her and sang to Her instead of the tyrannical and judgmental old God we were supposed to be worshipping. When I left, I expected to experience a lot of guilt and anxiety, but I didn't. I was one of the Goddess's women, and She welcomed me and I was at home.

—*Sylvia Sims*

A defining moment of my life was Easter week 1988 in Trapani, Sicily, when I watched the procession of the Black Madonna of Custonacci on Holy Thursday. Mesmerized by the spiral dance of men from the labor syndicates carrying the statue with a rocking, cradling gait of two steps backward and three steps forward, I looked about me and noted that the people along the route were in tears—and so was I. At the time, I knew that part of this emotional impact was the effect of the sirocco winds that blow in from Africa's Sahara Desert to the Sicilian shore. But subsequent events left me with the feeling that this was an assault of an ancient memory of the dark African Mother. Two days later, on my return to the American Academy in Rome, I dreamed of my own mother as a black Madonna. The next day, I learned she was dying of cancer. [The experience was so powerful, Lucia began writing a book about black Madonnas.]

Before the great urban fire of 1991 in Oakland, CA, I felt presentiments, anxieties, and free-floating fears that I could not explain. When the fire came, our home burned to the ground and I was beset by the feeling that the dark Mother had burned the house. My husband saved my manuscript on black Madonnas and we immediately began building a new home on the ashes of the old. Living in our radiant Mediterranean-style home (full of images of black Madonnas), I am conscious of the causal connection of the dark Mother with regeneration.

—*Lucia Chiavola Birnbaum*

My husband and I had begun to renew our relationship after being separated for nine months. I had just moved back into our house and was experiencing great sorrow and pain at being betrayed by people I had considered friends. I was also unsure that re-establishing the relationship with my husband was the right thing to do. In general, I was feeling unloved, used, abused, alone, helpless, and scared. I remember getting into bed and being overcome with great despair. I began to weep—the gut-wrenching, runny-nosed, body-rocking, pain-ridden, inconsolable type of weeping which I imagine accompanies the loss of a child.

My husband heard me and came in to the bedroom. He asked what was wrong and what did I want? I remember wailing that I wanted my Mother. He offered to call her but I answered that I did not want that mother. I wanted my Mother. Needless to say, that confused him and even in my distraught state, I realized I had no idea what I had meant. His further attempts to help me just made me more agitated and I told him to leave me alone. He left the room and I laid there a few more minutes rocking myself and sobbing.

Suddenly, I saw a woman before me. While she startled me, I felt no fear. She was dressed in an incredibly blue sari. Since my grandmother had been East Indian and she had passed out of this life years before, I asked if it was her. In answer to this question, an image of my grandmother dressed in the same sari and in the same pose appeared. Then the two images moved to become superimposed, one over the other. The two images did not match and did not line up with each other. When I realized that this was not my grandmother, her image disappeared immediately.

I asked the woman who she was and she said "Amma." At the sound of Her name, I was immediately calmed. I knew She was the Great Mother. I knew I was safe and warm.

I knew I was not alone. For the very first time in my life, I felt perfectly safe, loved, and nurtured. Since that moment, this realization has stayed with me. Even when I am experiencing something which is unpleasant—emotionally or physically—underneath it all I know that everything is OK. I know I am experiencing something which is only transitory. I know that there is a greater scope to it all and that the experience is only one minute piece of the whole picture.

I believe the Goddess appeared to me at that time in my life because I had spent the previous two years in a conscious and concentrated effort (both physically and spiritually) to open myself up for transformative change. Her appearance brought into focus the reality of Her existence. If She had previously made herself known to me in this manner, my methodical and rational Aquarian brain would have begun to look for proof of Her existence instead of accepting the experience as it happened.

I would not say that my philosophy changed drastically after my discovery of the Goddess but rather that Her appearance served as a catalyst for me to feel safe to publicly practice what I had always known to be true for me. Her appearance gave me the "safety net" I needed to be who I am and to be unafraid to speak my beliefs out loud.

—Valli Wasp

The word "Goddess" does not explain the feelings I associate with the event I'm going to describe. I cannot personalize such a strong force with the word Goddess and yet I know it was intensely female. When it happened, I had not even heard the word "Goddess."

When I turned fifty, I left my family responsibilities and went to Greece for three months to gather material for my next art show as a rite of passage in what I hoped would be a new section of my life. I had recently started to paint and exhibit seriously and with the thrill of limited success, I thought this was what I wanted to do for the rest of my life.

While roaming around the Greek islands, I stumbled on a group of archaeologists excavating on the remote island of Samothrace. They had taken over the only hotel on the island and my arrival was greeted with some suspicion until they realized I was an artist and not an archaeologist wanting to muscle in. I was invited to join them at night for dinners where we sat around a long narrow table and conversation flowed as freely as the retsina. There I learned much about the prehistory of the Aegean. One night, after many of my questions were answered by "we don't know that," the chief archaeologist said to one of his colleagues "You'd better show her the Earth-Mother rock."

Those words felt like a physical shock to me, an unexpected reaction. I couldn't wait to be taken to see this Earth-Mother rock at the deepest level of the dig, a spot which dated back to 2000 B.C.E. One of the young women took me there the next morning, pointed it out, and left me. It was a dark, egg-shaped rock, less than a meter high, with channels etched in it where libations had been poured. Alone, in the silence, I felt overcome with a power that seemed to emanate from it and I sat on a nearby slab of stone as if mesmerized. It seemed as if some force flowed over me as I sat there—for how long I don't know. The Earth-Mother was a whole new concept for me, but the message I was getting from this stone was the power of the feminine.

A beautiful turquoise lizard rustled at my feet and at last I stood up to leave, knowing I was carrying within me the seeds of change. I put my hand on the rock behind me to help myself up and I felt something brittle. I was astonished that it was a complete snake skin, quite beautiful, and I was sure it had not been there when I sat down. The snake is the symbol of renewal. That skin remained with me for many years before finally disintegrating.

Because of this experience, I became involved in a complete reappraisal of what it means to be female—not only my own femaleness but also the female impetus behind the social and spiritual development of the human race since (pre)historic times. I view things now with a wholeness and completeness not possible to me before. I also became angry at what had been done to women during the past few thousand years, and as I delved into prehistory, I felt compelled to write about my own discoveries. I could say I changed direction after that experience by writing instead of painting. But in retrospect, I realize that this is where I needed to go all the time.

Life is like a magnificent prism with a multitude of facets and we are capable of discovering only as many of them as our courage and imagination will allow. After my discovery of the female Divine, I felt a new world of understanding had opened for me.

—Dorothy Cameron

During the painful time of a relationship's ending, I turned more and more to meditation to quiet my tormented mind. One night when I walked into my Sufi meditation class, several women called out in chorus, "Janine, did you get Ammachi's blessing?"

"What's that?" I replied.

"Oh, if you haven't seen Amma yet, turn around now, get in your car and drive straight to the Community Center. Just go, and get Amma's blessing. You mustn't miss this."

Bewildered, I turned around. The center was less that a mile away, and a parking place materialized at the front door. As I stepped out of my car, a young woman with a baby ran into the building, and I was swept into her energy, following her all the way to the front of the crowded auditorium. There sat a small, plump, dark Indian woman in a white sari, embracing children and smiling radiantly. The woman with the infant knelt down on her knees, and The Mother enveloped her. I did likewise, and was instantly engulfed and flipped upside down as She held me powerfully, all the while kissing me and chanting strange sounds in my ear, pressing something shocking between my eyes, and into my hand.

A vast, inexpressible bliss overtook me as I flew from the room behind the woman and child, got into my car, and mindlessly ascended the hill toward home. Pulling into my garage, I opened the hand that still clutched the love-gift tightly. In my palm a chocolate candy kiss melted, and several red flower petals wafted fragrantly.

This was my first encounter with an incarnation of the Divine Mother, a human being who has fully realized the holy presence of the Mother within herself, and I knew it would take me a lifetime to understand this moment.

—Janine Canan

Initially, I didn't perceive what was happening as "Goddess." While still living in London, I became profoundly aware of the life and energies in the Earth, in the patterns of cosmos reflected in landscape, in the knowledge of our ancient ancestors, and in the vital role of the human in the link between cosmos and Earth. I became aware of the cycles of nature—sun, moon, stars, fertility, zodiac, elements, and directions. I began to celebrate these in dramatic and spectacular ritual performances.

When I moved to a little farm in East Anglia, I began to live these cycles in a very real, powerful, and day-to-day way. It was unbelievably intense, like waking from a dream into a clear reality. Yet it was wild and crazy and I felt I was being shattered into my component atoms, then restructured. It was then that I realized the being of "Goddess" within all this—the sun, the moon, the land, the trees, the Earth, the plants, the water, the stars, the sky—and that they (She) were (was) teaching me through a kind of direct transmission.

My performances became more personal, a kind of self-initiation into my woman magic, and the realm of Goddess. I was refinding everything I'd always known yet had somehow forgotten. This started when I was in my mid- to late-thirties and continued into my early forties. During much of this time, I rejected most of the modern world. I left my husband and children. I left the performance business I had created with my husband. I left all the personal possessions I had built up from childhood. In a sense, I left one identity and became another which felt more real and much more powerful. I stopped using my professional name and reverted to my birth name, which I liked for the first time in my life.

I could not bear to live with electricity. I got to the point where I couldn't even live in houses. I slept outdoors and began to walk, making journeys through the landscape between ancient sacred sites. I lived in caravans, traveled by horse and wagon, walked for 3½ months, then lived ten years in the Western Isles (of Scotland) with no electricity, no TV, very little of the modern world. I lived in a state of awareness of being part of the whole—at one with everything.

I had always hated myself and felt that everything wrong with my life was my fault, my inadequacy. I learned to love myself and see that what I had thought my weaknesses were my strengths. For a while, I was in limbo. It was quite a while before I performed the poetry I began to write or sold the pictures I began to create. I had my fourth child in a tipi with my feet on the Earth, with no medical people there. He was a son of the Goddess. I breast-fed him for 2 ¾ years and home-educated him until he was thirteen.

—Jill Smith

I discovered the Goddess when I had a glimpse of spirit, found it within myself, saw its power, and acknowledged it as a presence of the female Divine. As a result, I became deeply involved in the women's movement and, as I proceeded, my sculpture became a description of female energy and power.

I am still going through changes; life is about them for me. The changes are like removing the layers more and more to find the essential center and to understand the nature of the layers and what they mean.

—Nancy Azara

The Goddess manifested Herself in my life in surrealist fashion. I was writing my dissertation on *Surrealism in Contemporary Theater* at the time and was focused on writing a chapter on "The Women of Surrealism" when an extraordinary event occurred that transformed my life for over a decade.

On July 6, 1971, I was alone in my New York apartment working on an analysis and interpretation of the plays of Leonora Carrington, an important surrealist painter. At that time, there was no information on Leonora Carrington but I had come into contact with her plays, and I was determined to write about them. Since these plays dealt with characters from the realm of the dead and the spirit world, I could not fully understand them having only Freudian analysis available to me at the time. Jung was in disrepute back then.

Eventually I wrote to Leonora in Mexico, and she told me that absolutely nothing had been written about her works, and if I wanted to understand them, I would have to come to visit her in Mexico. As a graduate student with two daughters, I had limited funds, and could not make a trip to Mexico. But I got the idea that if I were to go to Greenwich Village, buy a Mexican dress, and put it on just as I was to do my writing, perhaps the vibrations from the dress would penetrate my bloodstream and illuminate my brain as to the meaning of her work.

On the evening of July 6, 1971, at about 6 p.m., I put on my dress, and uttered the following words: "If I can't go to Mexico, let Mexico come to me." No one was more astonished than I when the telephone rang, and a deep voice with an English accent announced to me "This is Leonora Carrington. I have just arrived from Mexico and I would like to meet you."

I was dumbfounded. I knew I had conjured her up. Or, as the surrealists would say, this was an example of *le hasard objectif,* objective chance, what we call synchronicity.

I told Leonora that she would never believe what had just happened, but, after hearing my story, she replied: "Of course I believe it, Gloria. I'm a witch!"

I was frightened. Then she invited me to meet with her at the Chelsea Hotel. There she was in full Mexican garb, looking particularly exotic because when she held up her hand, her fingers made the sign of the Horns of the Moon. When I asked her what that sign meant, she replied: "Those are the Holy Horns, Gloria!"

"The Holy Horns," I mumbled. "The Holy Horns of what?"

"The Holy Horns of Consecration," she boomed at me.

I remember I was shaking a lot because I had no idea what was happening. But I knew that a certain electricity was penetrating my entire being like a lightening rod. "Consecration of what?" I went on, perplexed.

"Consecration of the Goddess!" she roared to make certain that I would understand. But I had never heard of the Goddess in the singular. I had only heard about gods and goddesses. So I pursued my inquiry, like a typical graduate student.

"Who is the Goddess?" I challenged her.

"If you want to know who the Goddess is, Gloria, you will have to follow me to Europe. I am leaving in two days. As you travel with me, you will learn about the Goddess."

Although I could not go to Mexico, it just so happened I could go to Europe, for that very summer my husband was there doing research in physics. I met Leonora in Paris and the next summer, I went to Mexico where my Goddess education continued. When I arrived in Mexico, Leonora gave me two books to read. One was her unpublished novel, *The Hearing Trumpet*.

Not realizing what I had in my hands, I took my time in read–

ing it. When I got to the very last line in the novel, I gasped, for it read: "If the Old Woman can't go to Lapland, then Lapland must come to the Old Woman." That was the echo of the very sentence I had uttered about Mexico coming to me, the sentence that ultimately brought me into an encounter with the Celtic Goddess.

I asked Leonora why her 92-year-old heroine, living in an old age home in Mexico City, so yearned to go to Lapland (for I had no idea where Lapland was) and she replied quite nonchalantly: "Well, you see, Gloria, the Shamans of Lapland just happen to be the most magical people on Earth!'"

That was a sentence I was never to forget.

In January 1987, as I was organizing an ecofeminism conference at the University of Southern California, I received a phone call from a feminist professor from Norway, Berit Ås, who had founded the Feminist University outside Oslo. She was on a fundraising trip to the States, and her last stop was in California. She asked if she could stay with me. I had a very small apartment and suggested that she stay with another colleague but she insisted that she absolutely had to stay with me. Then I heard her talking to someone in the background, and she said: "Don't you want to know who I am traveling with?"

Naturally, I said I did. "I'm traveling with a shaman from Lapland, Gloria!" At those words I turned pale, and I began to quake. Unbelievable! That shaman must be the most powerful person on Earth for Leonora had proclaimed it.

Eventually it dawned on me that they were actually sent to stay with me. And so they both came to my office at USC and to my apartment. It was in my office that the young female shaman announced that she was next in line to head the shamanic lineage in Samiland (Lapland—northern sections of Norway, Sweden, Finland and the Kola peninsula of Russia). She told me "The Great Spirit has called you, Gloria. You must come to Samiland, walk 25 miles in nature and stay on a mountain to meet the Great Spirit." She also informed us that the Sami people have eight Goddesses and seven Gods. They also have a Triple Goddess Trinity. Their Goddesses have names that all end in "acca" such as Saracca, and these Goddesses are celebrated in sacred groves known as Accademias. Naturally, the Goddesses Acca would find me in Academia! It was completely logical.

I journeyed to Samiland, climbed their sacred mountains, visited their sacred sites, and partook in many rituals in honor of the Goddesses Acca.

Back in those days I was in an ecstasy about the Goddesses' presences in my life. I was in an ecstasy about shamanism, about the Sami, about ecofeminism. Now that I look back on all that ecstasy, I think I was in a permanently altered state of consciousness, perhaps a shamanic state of consciousness. In Samiland I saw spirits and heard the voices of the Sami ancestors speaking to me. I was "entranced"— in a trance. It never occurred to me that anything was wrong. But shamanism has a shadow side.

Over the next few years, all sorts of strange things happened to the Sami shaman and her family, culminating in the shaman's death. Soon afterwards, I became sick and manifested the same sorts of pains as the shaman had. No doctor could heal me. I looked for a healer and found a Jewish healer that I am still with.

I have always understood that it was men who created Judaism. However, today, feminist women are making changes towards a more egalitarian religion. I have made my peace with the religion to which I was born—for reasons that are part of the Great Mystery.

—*Gloria Orenstein*

I was raised on the Greek myths and the exploits of the Gods because my father wouldn't permit comic books or "little" stories like *The Bobbsey Twins Go to Denmark*. His idea of a good summer was copying the *Iliad* and the *Odyssey* in classical Greek.

Years late, rehearsing Euripides' *Trojan Women* and needing to understand Hecuba's frame of reference as she pounded the Earth and shouted to her ancestors "Do you see? Do you know? (what happened to women, to the women of Troy)," I started to search for answers. The first book I stumbled onto was entitled *Perseus and the Gorgon*. It was written to prove that Perseus had taken the head of the Gorgon statue from a temple in Corfu to bring back to mainland Greece.

I learned that the great Greek hero Perseus united Greece by destroying the temples, butchering and raping the priestesses and priests, and "by burying in oblivion and covering with silence the teaching of the Great Mother." That line had a deep, resounding influence in my life.

A passion was awakened to uncover these teachings, to know the Great Mother, to understand what happened. And this passion has never abated, fired by the writings and teaching of so many courageous women— Merlin Stone, Barbara Walker, Marija Gimbutas, Carol Christ, Cristina Biaggi, Vicki Noble, Elinor Gadon, Starhawk, Monica Sjöö,

Betty de Shong Meador, Mayatri Devi, and my mother. She taught me a Greek prayer to the Mother in Her incarnation as the Virgin that I have returned to over and over again.

> Give me Holy Mother
> Give me your help
> And never, never leave me
> Far from thee, Holy Mother

I never realized until I was much older that I had been praying to the Mother all those years, that my mother had set it up for me.

—*Olympia Dukakis*

Chapter Three

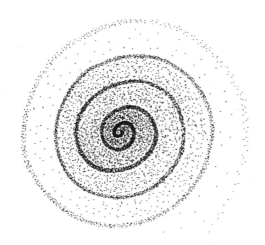

walking with the Goddess:
live, love, learn, laugh!

The planet desperately needs a balance.

—*Nancy Azara*

I think there is a great human hunger for a Divine Mother, for a caring Mother, and that we need this conceptualization of deity if we are to move away from the violent, punitive, and environmentally unsustainable dominator mode. So the Goddess is important not only for women but for men and children of both genders as a different way of imagining power, a more truly loving and humane way.

—*Riane Eisler*

Once women discover the power and fulfillment of Goddess experiences, they want and seek to continue their own growth and acceptance of Goddess and Mother Earth. They are usually surprised and overwhelmed by the love and caring they find.

I believe the entire world did and some parts still do know the Goddess.

—*Neen Namrae Lillquist*

Before I discovered the Goddess, I was aware of the Earth and of nature but did not actively work to make my life more in sync with Her. Now I have plants in almost every room of my house. I have gardens around my house. I recycle. And I do things like use cloth napkins rather than paper napkins. I sit and walk in nature as often as I can. I mourn for the beautiful willow tree that is dying in the yard next to mine. What is happening in nature seems closer than it did before.

—*Connie Dunn*

I feel as though I shed my skin every few months as I continually transform, become more loving and less judgmental, and take more responsibility for myself. I don't think there's anything more empowering for a woman than working directly with Goddess energy.

I think the Goddess is waking up! As co-creators of the Universe and of reality, we are waking Her up and She is awakening us.

—*Lori DeGayner*

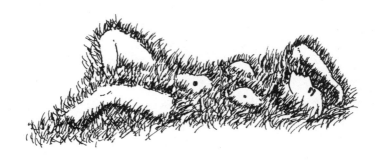

I believe that the Divine comes in many forms, and that the female Divine is emerging very powerfully at this crossroads of the millennium, a crossroads in our world view, and an ecosystem crisis. The Goddess offers guidance and direction on personal and collective levels. Prior to my dream of the Goddess], this philosophy would have seemed exceedingly strange to me, caught up as I was in the teaching of my childhood: God is a man, God is a man.

—*Patricia Healey McGovern*

The patriarchal religions seem to divide us, to hold humans up as superior over other forms of creation and, ultimately, to hold up certain groups of humans as superior over other groups. That isn't working. So for me, the practice of Goddess religion is a means of interconnecting, of restoring balance to the world.

—*Miriam Robbins Dexter*

I'm happy with my pagan spirituality, the way I can go to an ashram and a circle within the same week. I gravitate toward places that attempt to be open to the oneness of all, teaching principles that are more universal and not rigidly defined by dogma.

When I was a little girl, I thought it wonderful that I was a girl. I was so glad I didn't have a penis to get in the way of climbing trees and riding horses. So it intrigued me then, and continues to astonish me, that one gender is exalted above another. The Goddess did help me find my own strength but the inner core of my being still screams at the injustice and passivity. I believe in past lives and feel I must have been persecuted in one for such feelings.

As a child, I came into this world "knowing" we were all loved and connected. After a lecture by some nuns, I remember thinking that God must be sitting around with a big blackboard to write down all our "sins." This conflict between the knowledge that I came into this world with versus what I was taught created a wall that I continue to dismantle brick by brick.

The discovery of the Goddess is a revered part of my path through life. I continue to honor the Goddess yet do not do so exclusively. I feel the Divine can be found in a raindrop, the sun, a smile.

—*Lynne Fusco*

If we don't become very conscious of the principles of the Goddess in our lives, I think we'll probably see the end of it all. I think we need the Goddess to heal us. We need female energy to balance what has gone on for millennia before us. We need it to expand our consciousness. As a planet, we are at the point of near exhaustion. But we have to go all the way down in order for us to come back up. That's what the myth of Demeter and Persephone is about. I think this is our collective dying process.

—*Charoula Dontopoulos*

I think the Earth is tired in many ways. The big trees are going, not just being sawed down but going. The oak trees are falling from storms and dying. Every day there is another one gone and this urban sprawl and these little artificial houses that are not even made out of real materials are taking over the countryside. People aren't connected to the Earth although I think they will be again, especially with the coming of solar technology and wholesome food.

—*Gail Dunlap*

I'm not at all sure there is a point to existence but if there is, it is to enjoy the Earth plane. I believe we are here to experience a physical life form and I believe the plan is to experience abundance, not an oppressive, abusive reality centered in scarcity, hierarchy, and fear.

It is clear to me that the Judeo-Christian world of the West, where I live, is one which was developed out of a desert mindset, a place of scarcity.

That world view is based on the belief in an ascendant deity who is separate from us and the Earth, and "more" than we are. This has created hierarchy, and promotes "power over." And this male thing: no archetypes of divine women except Mary. What a setup. I don't buy it now and I never did.

—*Patricia Cuney*

As a child, I remember going to a doctor in Manhattan with my mother. The doctor had an Asian-style painting of a surgeon performing brain surgery on a patient. Under the painting, which was anonymous, were the words "A life lived for others is a life well spent." This made a great and lasting impression on me and I have always wanted to help others. But I had to learn that the Goddess is inside me and that by helping only others and not myself my life would be out of balance. I needed to learn to worship and bring flowers to my internal Goddess.

In my work, I meet many women who make this same mistake. As they care for children, husbands, households, elderly parents, etc., they do not stop to honor themselves. It took a long time for me to make this discovery. It took both illness and recovery to discover my true nature.

I saw Her (the Goddess) in me and took the responsibility of being Her living representative. And this brought a much needed balance to my daily life.

I am the Goddess!

—Susan Menje

We are coming into the time of the violet ray, the energy of Venus, and the eight-pointed star, all of which are Hers. It is a wonder and mystery to be alive, a privilege to be incarnated. It is possible to accomplish anything one sets one's mind, heart and will to fully— that "fully" is the trick. My father taught me that and I've come to believe it through my own experience. Knowing the Goddess has helped me feel at home and safe in this world. Because of my initiation, I know in my bones and heart that She is always there for me.

—Melinda Gardiner

I think the Goddess is coming forth now because She has to. Our culture has gone as far as it can without Her, to the point of self-destructing, and needs to remember how to honor life, and how to relate to a Mystery beyond its definitions.

—Cassia Berman

As our world is threatened by enormous depredation, it is important to remember that this globe is our Mother, our source and protector, sustenance and re-absorber, the living body of the Divine Source of all.

The Hindus tell a story of Lord Shiva, inebriated and selfishly absorbed, slapping his spouse, the Mahadevi. He tries to flee Her anger but she appears in every possible direction, eventually swallowing him with the warning: Whoever injures the Source of Nature injures himself. Shiva awakens from his stoned stupor with the red slap mark of his hand on his own face.

I take comfort that more people seem aware of the presence of the Goddess in the environment around them, in each other, and in themselves. Hopefully we can turn back the tide of greed, self-centeredness, rampant neglect, and destruction of this green planet who is our Mother.

—*Len Rosenberg*

It is the time of the Goddess. I've been teaching for 15 years and I'm seeing more and more women desiring the drum but not understanding why. Because I connect the drum with the Goddess, with the Mother, I feel it is just Her time.

We in Western culture have been colonized. We've been done to and now we're undoing. And I thank the Goddess that She is expressed in other cultures so that we have the mirroring and the imagery we need, that all is not lost. Outside the U.S., the Goddess is still quite present.

—*Ubaka Hill*

The Goddess represents a nurturing, caring universe. No mother would let one child eat and another starve, one wear silk and the other rags. She would not foul up her own nest.

Those values have disappeared and need to be rediscovered. (I know, duh, beat your head against the wall.) To me, it's better to beat my head against the wall than to spend the rest of my physical existence with blinders on. I'd rather chance the blood.

—*Lucy Harrison*

I think, under patriarchy, we have just about used up our options. It will take a major shift in thinking (and acting) to assure a world in which we can all live. Perhaps, on some level, the reason so many people are experiencing the Goddess is that our survival instincts are kicking in. We are searching for something more, something better, something we once had but lost along the way. This big shift may be the growth and development of the baby boomer. We're reaching midlife and now our souls require us to search for more.

—*Karen London*

We're in a moment where things are coming together in synthesis. I hope that patriarchy is having its last gasp. Certainly the devastation of the planet lets us know that it should be the last gasp.

I feel that we are at the time of the last curtain call, a command performance. We're all here, all the souls are in.

We've pretty much destroyed the natural balance of the environment but I have no fear for the planet because I think She has easy ways of healing herself. I actually think the microbes will probably bring the planet back into balance and we may not survive that. And there are ways the natural healing forces will take over and right the wrong.

It's an incredible moment because of the terrible choices that are being made about things such as biogenetic engineering. The polar ice caps are melting, the ozone layer is gone, the volcanoes are all fixing to go off. It's happening and we're in it.

—*Vicki Noble*

I see more clearly and deeply how to hold the form of the Spirit without despair about destruction. Accepting tumultuous change as a necessary part of planetary shift. That too is "Goddess" at work.

I see things as they are and know that change is necessary and open ended. I am more hopeful because this spiritual dimension holds such power.

—*Suzanne Bellamy*

Earth is forcing things from the unconscious of the human race and what's coming up is sheer life survival. I think we're tuned in but I also think the force is coming up and grabbing us, taking us by the throat as it were, volcanically contacting us.

—*Starr Goode*

I now realize that all the history and religious books have been just some man's interpretation, politically or financially arranged piles of words. None of it ever made sense to me—the wars, the pain, the poverty, the oppression of people or animals or plants. Now I believe the way of the Goddess, the peace, plenty and respect for life as well as what we perceive as inanimate, is the way the Earth needs to go.

—Hope Kasley Rendell Harvey

I believe we need to join together to take responsibility for the suffering in our community and our world—for those who are hungry, ill, unhoused, unloved, uneducated, imprisoned, unheard. The needless death or suffering of any of us diminishes us all.

I believe in the sacramental dimension of the home, of sharing food and drink, of lovemaking, of friendships, and the community of all creatures, of solitude and memory. I believe in my/our connections with the Earth, with flowering and shedding, with the waxing and waning of the moon, the coming closer to and then distancing from the sun, a child's hand in mine, an elder leaning on my arm.

The Way of Life seems to me a treasure hunt where I must not be blinded to the clues or the treasure by expectations.

—Karen Ethelsdattar

It is imperative that female energy be awakened in both men and women at this time because the potential for global annihilation is at its most critical point. The destruction we need to heal is not limited to the physical damage which has been done to Mother Earth but also includes the spiritual, emotional, and physical damage which we have allowed or have inflicted on each other.

—*Valli Wasp*

Human beings have reached a turning point in planetary existence. If we continue the narrow consciousness of protecting ourselves and our loved ones at the expense of all others, our planet will become uninhabitable.

—*Suzanne Zuckerman*

This is the Earth rising up to fight for Herself through us. The Goddess is that part that is not transcendent, that is imminent, that is in every leaf. The patriarchal God was taken from Earth and transcended into the heavens, and I think that was a mistake because it removed us from the reality of our behavior here on Earth. This is where we are, this is where we must find heaven, or create heaven.

—*Catherine Allport*

You ask, are we still going through changes? I am—it's constant. I look forward to the time I know wholeness, unity with every breath and breadth of my being, where there is no polarity, no form and formlessness, no feminine or masculine.

—*Diana Marto*

Our Earth is going through a long, difficult healing process and Gaia needs us to heal the abused child, the slaughtered animal, the poisoned river, the conflict within our homes, the conflict within our communities, the conflicts between regions of the planet. She needs our alert and sensitive awareness, our efforts to heal ourselves, our efforts to educate ourselves and others, our action. She is crying out and we are crying with Her, even if we don't know what it is that is making us uncomfortable, sad, depressed, angry, in pain, in grief. There is much grief work to be done and much healing too.

—*Eva Yaa Asantewaa*

I find that now I am more trusting of my intuition, my inner voices. I'm willing to believe and act without documented fact—I didn't always have that courage.

I trust that I am changing and growing—not to do so would be death. Now I'm able to let it happen to me.

—*Sally Hamburger*

Appendices

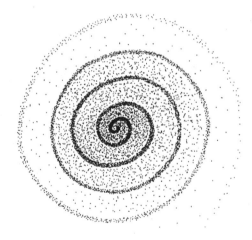

Who's Who

These are very short biographies of the terrific people who contributed to *In the Footsteps of the Goddess.*

Catherine Allport is a photographer and an environmental activist living in California.

Eva Yaa Asantewaa is a psychic and energy healing practitioner who lives in New York City.

Nancy Azara is a sculptor and healer who lives in New York City.

Sandra Barnhouse has been a university publications editor for twenty years. Currently she works as a freelance artist and is developing an accessory product line under the label YYKEES. Her spare time is spent researching early Celtic queens of Britain. She lives in Minnesota.

Suzanne Bellamy is an artist and writer who lives in Australia.

Agathe Bennich was born in Sweden and now lives in California where she paints and teaches art history and studio art at San Francisco City College.

Kristina Berggren was born in Sweden but raised in Italy. She is an archaeologist who now lives in California.

Cassia Berman teaches T'ai chi chu'an and qi gong and has been a practitioner of the Chinese healing arts for over 20 years. She lives in upstate New York.

Lucia Chiavola Birnbaum was a founder of the Peace and Freedom Party in 1967. She is an independent scholar who focuses on the history of oppressed peoples, and the author of *Black Madonnas: Feminism, Religion, and Politics,* published in Italy. She lives in California.

Mary Brenneman is a writer and teacher. She co-authored *Crossing the Circle at the Holy Wells of Ireland* with her husband Ted and taught anthropology at Johnson State College in Vermont.

Dorothy Cameron is a writer and painter living in Australia.

Dr. Janine Canan is a psychiatrist and a poet living in California.

Christopher Castle is a painter, printmaker, and composer living in California.

Christopher is a massage therapist living in the southeastern United States.

Joan Cichon is a reference librarian, history instructor, and writer who lives in Illinois.

Glenda Cloughley is a therapist and writer living in Australia.

Patricia Cuney recently received her law degree from the University of Texas. She is the founder of WomanSpirit, a non-profit educational corporation which produced conferences on the Goddess, and lives in Texas.

Lori DeGayner is a secretary who works closely with the Re-formed Congregation of the Goddess in Madison, Wisconsin.

Dr. Miriam Robbins Dexter is a writer and professor of comparative mythology at the University of California at Los Angeles. She wrote *Whence the Goddesses,* and edited and supplemented *The Living Goddess,* the last book written by Marija Gimbutas.

Charoula Dontopoulos is an activist and founded several feminist periodicals in New York and Greece. After a bout with cancer, she became interested in the healing professions and is now a Polarity and Reiki master and an accomplished herbalist. She lives in Ohio and Greece.

Imogene Drummond is an artist, writer, and designer who lives in upstate New York.

Olympia Dukakis is a well-known actress on stage and screen. She won an Academy Award for best supporting actress for her work in *Moonstruck.*

Gail Dunlap is an ardent environmentalist and has restored an extensive wetland as well as a 19th-century log cabin. She is also a poet, painter, and animal rights activist.

Connie Dunn is a writer and storyteller who lives in Texas.

Riane Eisler is the author of two international bestsellers, *The Chalice and the Blade* and *Sacred Pleasures,* as well as other books. She is president of the Center for Partnership Studies in Pacific Grove, California.

Karen Ethelsdattar is retired from working at an international student center, the Women's Ordination Conference, two seminaries, a church, and a Jewish magazine. She now lives in New Jersey and publishes her own poetry.

Jean Freer has been a practicing priestess, a school teacher, a Tarot practitioner, the founder of the Feminist Archives, and now runs a holistic health center. She lives in California.

Lynne Fusco is a school psychologist and a holistic psychotherapist, living in New Jersey.

Melinda Gardiner is a registered nurse working in community health. She is also a musician, and produces events featuring traditional music, particularly Celtic music. She lives in upstate New York.

Starr Goode is a poet living in California. She worked on one of the first feminist newspapers, and hosted the first cable television show in Los Angeles on the Goddess, *The Goddess in Art*.

Sally Hamburger is a historian living in Delaware. She is the program coordinator for her Univesalist Church and is involved with Opera Delaware.

Barbara Harrell is discovering the world through changed eyes, dancing the dance of life, and enjoying every minute of it.

Lucy Harrison is a maverick and a dreamer and would rather travel down the path no one is using. She is proud of her five warm, caring, beautiful children who share her beliefs.

Hope Kasley Rendell Harvey runs an alternative health practice in New Jersey. She is a Reiki master and an Amma therapist.

Beth Hensperger is a writer living in California.

Hera is an artist, poet, and real estate developer living in upstate New York.

Ubaka Hill is a renowned drummer and teacher. She lives in upstate New York.

Mary Hopkins is a writer and lecturer on women's culture, the visual arts, literature, anthropology, archaeology, and psychology. She is now retired and lives in Pennsylvania.

Patricia Hubbard lives on an island off the coast of Maine where she makes pots, contemplates, and tends dreams.

Jade cofounded the Re-formed Congregation of the Goddess. She is a copublisher of the oldest women's spirituality newspaper in the U.S., *Of a Like Mind,* and administers the Women's Thealogical Institute. She lives in Wisconsin.

Linda Johnsen is a writer and editor whose books include *The Living Goddess* and *Daughters of the Goddess.* She lives in northern California.

Judith Johnson is an artist and professor of the humanities who lives in Pennsylvania.

Neen Namrae Lillquist lives on a farm in Minnesota. She recently retired from a career as a nursing administrator which included work in Brazil, Pakistan, and Nepal.

Mimi Lobell lives in New York City and is a professor of architecture at Pratt Institute. She is a widely acclaimed authority on Goddess temples and on symbolism in art and architecture.

Karen London has been a nurse, and directed a women's resource center. She is now pursuing a degree in women's studies. She lives in Maryland.

Ayo Maat is a poet, writer, editor, storyteller, and community activist who lives in Illinois.

Tatyana Mamonova was exiled from the Soviet Union for her feminist beliefs. She is a poet and artist and has written several books about Russian feminism. She started the periodical *Women and Earth* which combines writings and art by American and Russian feminists. She now lives in New York City.

Joan Marler is a teacher, lecturer, and writer who lives in California. She edited *In the Realm of the Ancestors,* published by Knowledge, Ideas & Trends, and is working on a biography of Marija Gimbutas.

Diana Marto is a performance artist and dancer. She lives in California.

Patricia Healey McGovern is a writer living in upstate New York.

Susan Menje is an artist, a high priestess in Wicca, and the executive producer of a radio talk show. She is developing an on-line magazine called *The Lotus Speaks*. She lives in New York City.

Julie Forest Middleton is a publisher, and the editor of *Songs for Earthlings*. She lives in Pennsylvania.

Vicki Noble is a healer, teacher, and author of a number of books, including *Motherpeace* with Karen Vogel. She also wrote *Down Is Up with Aaron Eagle* about her son who has Down's Syndrome. She lives in California.

Gloria Orenstein is a professor of comparative literature and women's studies at the University of Southern California. She is the author of several books, including *The Reflowering of the Goddess.* She lives in California.

Len Rosenberg worked for many years as a civil servant in New York City. He is currently retired and still lives in the city.

Lydia Ruyle is an artist and a faculty member in the department of visual arts at the University of Northern Colorado. She also teaches at the Columbia Center for Book and Paper Arts in Chicago. She lives in Colorado.

Sylvia Sims co-founded Astarte Shell Press, a publisher dedicated to bringing out works of feminist, spiritual, theological, and economic justice. She is now a licensed practical nurse and a freelance editor living in Maine.

Monica Sjöö is an artist and writer, author of *The Great Cosmic Mother.* She lives in England.

Jill Smith is a poet, writer, and lecturer. She lives in England.

Jenny Badger Sultan is an artist and teacher at City College of San Francisco. She lives in California.

Valli Wasp owns a computer consulting business and is copublisher of *Light Voices*. She lives in Texas.

Terry Whye is a potter with her own studio. She lives in Maryland.

Donna Wilshire reclaims the oral tradition with a one-woman performance piece in which she tells stories from early woman-honoring, nature-revering times. She is the author of *Virgin, Mother, Crone: Myths and Mysteries of the Triple Goddess* and *Alleloo! The Virgin's Child Dies and Is Born Again! Myths and Mysteries of the Sacred Blood*.

Suzanne Zuckerman is a teacher of English in special education in New York City and is the author of three novels and numerous short stories, plays, and articles. She lives in New York City.

Archaeological Research and the Great Goddess

I believe that most of the world enjoyed a pre-patriarchal period during which women were respected, even revered, and people worshipped a numinous power they identified as female. I base this belief on compelling evidence found in pre-patriarchal, matristic societies throughout the world. In some regions—Europe, the Eastern Mediterranean, parts of Asia—the information is abundant and has been thoroughly studied. In other areas such as China and the Americas, evidence is sparse or has not been systematically examined. However, this situation has been changing as new findings emerge in support of matristic societies, based primarily on archaeological remains from the Paleolithic period (35,000 B.C.E.).

With the discovery of the Har Kar Khoum site in Israel by Italian archaeologist Emmanuele Anati, which dates to 45,000 B.C.E., the inception of the Paleolithic period is being pushed back. The Har Kar Khoum site is now considered the oldest religious sanctuary in the world. In addition, a group of maverick prehistorians from the Netherlands believe there is evidence among our Neanderthal forebears of worship of a female deity from the

Lower Paleolithic period, approximately 500,000 B.C.E. Even before the advent of our own species, *Homo sapiens,* in 35,000 B.C.E., our Neanderthal ancestors placed triangular stones over burials, engraved cup marks, and, in some cases, carved female figurines.

Evidence for an archaic female divinity has also been suggested through anthropological analogy, and from the mythology of societies that, until recently, lived in a Paleolithic state of existence. Based on the archaeological record and from mythology, we can assume that early matristic societies enjoyed an egalitarian existence, expressed their artistic natures, basked in a spiritually rich life, worshipped a female deity, and had no warfare.

In most parts of the world, the Neolithic (7000-2500 B.C.E.) was overwhelmingly female-centered. The eminent and pioneering archaeologist Marija Gimbutas said, "The Neolithic *is* the Goddess." During the Neolithic period, people lived in self-sufficient villages, towns, and even cities, practiced agriculture and irrigation, the domestication of animals, pottery, spinning and weaving, astronomy, plumbing, writing, and metallurgy. Neolithic societies were egalitarian, consisting of matrilineal families tracing their clan lines through the mother. Women had high status but men were not subordinate. There is *no indication of war* in the early Neolithic—weaponry, fortifications, and images of battle in art are absent. Female figurines predominate in the Neolithic. The male

appears later as a musician, athlete, worshipper, thinker, or nature god. The Goddess in Her different aspects seems to have been universally worshipped. She was an agricultural goddess as well as a sky goddess, a mother goddess, and a death and regeneration goddess. She was associated with a number of animals including the bird and snake (Her aerial and earthly manifestations), the cow, pig, and bee.

During the Neolithic period, society and culture changed from matristic to patriarchal in many regions of the world. According to Marija Gimbutas, in southwestern Europe this change occurred as a result of three waves of invading, warlike nomads, the Kurgans, who originated near the Caspian Sea. This conclusion has been substantiated by geneticist Luigi Cavalli Sforza of the University of California at Los Angeles, by the Russian archaeologist Nicolai Merpert, and by marine biologists Bill Ryan and Walter Pittman in their book *Noah's Flood*. These invaders were pastoralists and worshipped a sky god. According to Riane Eisler in *The Chalice and the Blade,* these warlike nomads worshipped the blade as opposed to the chalice, placing a higher value on taking life than giving it.

This change was more gradual in other regions of the world, such as China, but it did occur. Whether by conquest or gradual encroachment, this change from egalitarian and matristic to hierarchical and male-dominated societies meant women lost their status, often becoming property. It also meant the existing Earth- or Goddess-based spirituality was supplanted by religions centered around a God of the shining sky and his warlike pantheon.

But vestiges of the old belief system lingered in societies throughout the world in art, mythology, and folklore. Through the efforts of early researchers and writers, especially the work of Marija Gimbutas, we began to uncover and document the roots of the Goddess religion in the Paleolithic and Neolithic periods. Professor Gimbutas's contributions to a complete understanding of the Goddess and the possibilities of matristic societies have been invaluable. Her meticulous archaeological research and her revolutionary interpretation of the material set down roots from which scientific research and female-centered spirituality can blossom. Because of Professor Gimbutas's archaeological contributions, the historical aspect of the Goddess movement has been firmly documented, and its spiritual aspect, which inspired this book, is starting to flourish. These two aspects of the Goddess movement need to co-exist to help us reclaim our female power and re-establish a balance between the sexes.

The re-emergence and development of women's spirituality is crucial for human consciousness and for our planet because it stipulates a consideration for the Earth itself as a living, breathing being, a spiritual being. Moreover, this understanding of the Earth is critical because it calls for a sacred regard for all its inhabitants—animals and plants—without which we will all perish spiritually and physically.

—*Cristina Biaggi*

A Time Line of the Goddess in History

ALL DATES ARE APPROXIMATE

Europe

 UPPER PALEOLITHIC GATHERERS AND HUNTERS

 APPROXIMATELY 33,000 B.C.E. VENUS OF WILLENDORF AUSTRIA

30,000 B.C.E. GREAT CAVE PAINTINGS CHAUVET, FRANCE

Eastern Mediterranean

45,000-35,000 B.C.E. HAR KAR KHOUM SANCTUARY ESTABLISHED IN ISRAEL

Africa

5 MILLION YEARS AGO HUMAN BEINGS EVOLVED IN OLDUVAI, AFRICA

 UPPER PALEOLITHIC ERA ENGRAVINGS OF WILD ANIMALS ON SAHARA CLIFFS AND NILE VALLEY

Asia

UPPER PALEOLITHIC ERA GATHERERS/HUNTERS THROUGHOUT ASIA

 UPPER PALEOLITHIC FEMALE FORMS AROUND LAKE BAIKAL

UPPER PALEOLITHIC CAVE PAINTINGS IN KAPOCA CAVE, URALS

Americas

APPROXIMATELY **20,000** B.C.E. FIRST PEOPLE MIGRATE FROM ASIA AND POSSIBLY FROM EUROPE TO THE AMERICAS

Australia

50,000 B.C.E., POSSIBLY **120,000** B.C.E. FIRST HUMANS IN AUSTRALIA

40,000 B.C.E. ROCK ENGRAVINGS IN OPEN SITES AND CAVE PAINTINGS OF RED OCHRE AND BLOOD IN CENTRAL AUSTRALIA AND NORTHERN TERRITORY (LAURIE CREEK)

A Time Line of the Goddess in History

ALL DATES ARE APPROXIMATE

Europe

LATE PALEOLITHIC
LA MAGDELAINE
IN FRANCE

10,000 B.C.E.
HUMANOID FIGURES
PAINTED ON PEBBLES
IN MAS D'AZIL

10,000–7000 B.C.E.
PAINTINGS ON ROCK
SHELTERS IN SPAIN TO
AFRICA

Eastern Mediterranean

10,000 B.C.E.
PLASTERED SKULLS AND FIGURINES
IN JERICHO

Africa

7000-3000 B.C.E..
TASSILI CULTURE IN
ALGERIA

4000 B.C.E.
TASSILI HORNED GODDESS
IN ALGERIA

Asia

UPPER PALEOLITHIC ERA
BIRD GODDESS IN
MAL'TA, SIBERIA

11,000 B.C.E. - 300 A.D.
JOMON CULTURE
IN JAPAN

Americas

11,000 B.C.E.
MOBILIER ART AND ROCK ART
IN CLOVIS, NEW MEXICO

Australia

14,000 B.C.E.
STENCILED HANDS
IN TASMANIA

12,000 B.C.E.
ENGRAVING
IN OLARY

A Time Line of the Goddess in History

ALL DATES ARE APPROXIMATE

Europe

 7TH MILENNIUM
HUNDREDS OF
FEMALE FIGURES IN
LEPENSKI VIR IN THE
FORMER YUGOSLAVIA

6TH MILENNIUM
FEMALE FIGURES IN
AEGEAN

 6TH MILENNIUM
FEMALE FIGURES IN
VINÇA

Eastern Mediterranean

 6TH MILENNIUM
ENTHRONED BIRTH GODDESS
IN ÇATAL HÜYÜK, TURKEY

6TH MILENNIUM
MOTHER GODDESS
IN TEPE SARAB, IRAN

Africa

 5TH MILENNIUM
BIRD GODDESS
IN PREDYNASTIC EGYPT

Asia

6TH MILENNIUM
GYLANDRIC SOCIETIES AND
YANGSHAO CULTURE IN
(e.g. BAMPO VILLAGE) CHINA

 5TH MILENNIUM
MIDDLE JOMON CULTURE
IN JAPAN

Americas

 4TH MILENNIUM
FEMALE FIGURE WITH CHILD IN
VALDIVIA, CENTRAL AMERICA

 2ND MILENNIUM
FEMALE FIGURE IN
TLATICO, MEXICO

Australia

 8TH TO 6TH MILENNIUM
QUEENSLAND PETROGLYPHS
IN LAURA

 8TH MILENNIUM
RAINBOW SERPENT PRESENTED
AS FEMALE AT THE DJUWARR
SITE, ARNHEIM

A Time Line of the Goddess in History

ALL DATES ARE APPROXIMATE

Europe

4TH MILENNIUM FEMALE FIGURES IN MALTA

4TH MILENNIUM FEMALE FIGURE IN ARENE CANDIDE, ITALY

4TH MILENNIUM FEMALE FIGURES IN FRANCE

Eastern Mediterranean

6TH MILLENNIUM FEMALE FIGURES IN ANATOLIA

6TH MILLENNIUM EYE GODDESS IN BRAK, SYRIA

4TH MILENNIUM LILITH FIGURE IN SUMER

Africa

4TH TO 1ST MILLENNIUM DYNASTIC ART IN EGYPT

Asia

4TH MILENNIUM YANGSHAO CULTURE IN CHINA

4TH MILENNIUM HINDUS VALLEY CIVILIZATION (MOHENJO DARO) IN INDIA

Americas

2ND MILENNIUM FEMALE FIGURE WITH CAT HEAD IN POVERTY POINT, LOUISIANA

2ND MILENNIUM FEMALE FIGURE IN VENEZUELA

Australia

7000 B.C.E. FEMALE HUNTER IN ARNHEM LAND

A Time Line of the Goddess in History

ALL DATES ARE APPROXIMATE

Europe

 4TH MILLENNIUM FEMALE FIGURES IN PORTUGAL

2ND MILENNIUM SNAKE GODDESS IN CRETE

2ND MILENNIUM FEMALE FIGURES CYCLADIC ISLANDS, AEGEAN

2ND MILENNIUM FEMALE FIGURE IN YUGOSLAVIA

Eastern Mediterranean

 3RD MILLENNIUM FEMALE FIGURE IN MARI, MESOPOTAMIA

2ND MILLENNIUM MANY LATE FEMALE FIGURINES FOUND THROUGHOUT EASTERN MEDITERRANEAN

Africa

 2ND MILLENNIUM FEMALE FIGURE IN NUBIA

2ND MILLENNIUM ART MADE OF PERISHABLE MATERIALS IN REGIONS OTHER THAN EGYPT

Asia

3RD MILLENNIUM ARRIVAL OF INDO-EUROPEANS IN INDIA

3RD TO 2ND MILLENNIUM ESTABLISHMENT OF PATRIARCHAL DYNASTIES IN CHINA AND JAPAN

Americas

 3RD MILLENNIUM FEMALE FIGURE IN ECUADOR

2ND MILLENNIUM FEMALE FIGURE FROM OLMECS CULTURE IN MEXICO

2ND MILLENNIUM PREDOMINANTLY FEMALE FIGURINES FOUND IN MOST CULTURES IN THE AMERICAS

Australia

ART ON ROCK SHELTERS (CHAMBERS GORGE) AND IN CAVES THROUGHOUT AUSTRALIA

2ND TO 1ST MILLENNIUM X-RAY PAINTING STYLE IN ARNHEM LAND

Glossary of Terms

Anatolia: The ancient name for Turkey

Ashram: A religious retreat for a colony of disciples

Beltane: The first day of summer in the ancient Celtic calendar, celebrated on May 1, and one of the two major festival days in the Wiccan calendar. Its opposite in the year is Samhain, celebrated on November 1. Beltane is the great festival of fertility often celebrated with bonfires and dancing.

Budapest, Z (Zsuzanna): Author (see suggested readings) of many books on women's spirituality, founder of the first feminist witches coven (Susan B. Anthony Coven Number 1), and founder of a religion known as Dianic Witchcraft, a separatist, women-only religion. Z Budapest was one of the first women to speak, write, and encourage woman-based spirituality in the United States.

Buddhism: A religion of Eastern and Central Asia which grew out of the teachings of Gautama Buddha and which postulates that suffering is inherent in life and that one can escape it into nirvana by mental and moral self-purification.

Çatal Hüyük: One of the largest early Neolithic towns in the world, located on the Konya plateau in south-central Turkey and dating from the end of the 8th millennium B.C.E. The excavated portion of this site has mud-brick houses, temples, wall paintings and reliefs, sculptures and a host of other objects which strongly suggest an egalitarian, gylandric society.

Chakra: Psychic centers of the body prominent in the physiological practices of certain forms of Hinduism and Buddhism. There are seven chakras, each associated with a specific color, shape, sense organ, natural element, and deity.

Chicago, Judy: A groundbreaking, internationally recognized American artist famous for feminist installations such as "The Dinner Party" and "The Birth Project."

Craft, The: see Wicca

Eleusis: A town located in Attica, Greece, which was the center of annual rituals known as the Eleusinian Mysteries conducted in honor of Demeter and Persephone. The celebration of the Mysteries continued to the end of the 4th century A.D. The earliest sanctuary at Eleusis antedated the 7th century B.C.E.

Gimbutas, Marija: An eminent, world-renowned archaeologist. Her excavations of Neolithic sites in southeastern Europe led her to a detailed study of the earliest agrarian cultures (6500–3500 B.C.E.) of that continent. The traditions of these cultures were peaceful, egalitarian, profoundly spiritual, and aesthetically refined. Women and children were honored and the cyclical powers of nature were worshipped and expressed in thousands of female images. Gimbutas started a new discipline called archaeomythology, an interdisciplinary approach to scholarship combining archaeology, mythology, folklore, linguistics, and anthropology. Professor Gimbutas challenged traditional assumptions about the patriarchal origins of Western civilization. Her "Kurgan Hypothesis," which explains the transition to Indo-Europeanized, patriarchal cultures, has been a center of scholarly debate for over 40 years.

Green Tara: see Tara

Gylandric: A term coined by author Riane Eisler and used by archaeologist Marija Gimbutas to refer to a society where women and men are equal. From the Greek root words "gyn" (woman) and "andros" (man).

Hinduism: A complex body of social, cultural, and religious beliefs and practices which evolved in the Indian subcontinent. Hinduism is characterized by the caste system and acceptance of the Veda as the most sacred text. The goal of Hinduism is liberation (nirvana) from the cycle of rebirth and the suffering brought about by one's own actions (karma).

Kali: Hindu Goddess whose name translates as both "dark" and "time." She is the Goddess from whom all are born and to whom all must return. She is actively worshipped in India.

Kundalini: A form of yoga which starts with the belief that a latent power called "kundalini" (another name for Kali) lies coiled like a snake at the base of the spine. One practices Kundalini yoga for the explicit purpose of awakening this force and increasing one's psychic powers.

Magna Dea: Great Goddess, from Latin "magna" (great) and "dea" (Goddess). The Magna Dea of Çatal Hüyük is the Birthing Goddess flanked by lions.

Mantra: In Hinduism, an invocation used in worship. This invocation may be in the form of a brief petition or the repetition of a sacred word.

Mastristic societies: As defined by archaeologist Marija Gimbutas, these are societies in which women are honored but men are not subjugated.

Meditation: An engaging in serious reflection; keeping the mind in a state of contemplation. There are many ways to meditate. One is to close the eyes and concentrate on the breath as a way of quieting the mind and becoming more in tune with the cosmos.

Mobilier art: A term usually used in reference to transportable Paleolithic art objects. Often used in contrast to the term "parietal art" which refers to reliefs or wall paintings.

Pythia of Delphi: The oracular high priestess of Delphi, one of the most important sacred centers of ancient Greece.

Sabbat: The origin of the word *sabbat* and its meaning is somewhat controversial, depending on the source of information used. It is generally thought to be a corruption of the word "sabbath" coined during the Inquisition by clerics and others on witch hunts. A sabbat, they maintained, was the devil's mockery of church holy days.

Others maintain that "sabbat" had its own meaning prior to the Inquisition and that it signified festival days celebrated by pagans.

There are eight sabbats in all. The four major festival days are Beltane (May 1), Lammas or Lughnasadh (August 1), Samhain (November 1), and Oimelc (February 1). The four minor sabbats are the equinoxes of spring and fall and the solstices of summer and winter.

Samhain: A Gaelic word meaning "summer's end," celebrated on November 1, the beginning of summer being Beltane or May 1. Together, Samhain and Beltane form an ancient division of the year into summer and winter. Nowadays, Samhain is considered the year's most important holiday for witches and is filled with rituals honoring deceased loved ones. Since ancient tradition called for the start of festivals on the evening before, Samhain begins on October 31, Halloween. A day to honor the dead was celebrated in ancient cultures as far removed from each other as Egypt and pre-Spanish Mexico.

Shakti, Shaktism: Shakti, also known as Parvati, is the female principle, the Great Goddess, and the wife of Shiva in Hinduism. Followers of Shaktism honor the female traditions embodied in Hinduism.

Shiva: The destroyer or regeneration aspect of the Hindu trinity which also includes Brahma, the creator, and Vishnu, the preserver. Shiva is also the husband of Shakti.

Solstice: The two days of the year, the first days of summer and winter, which are marked when the sun's rays strike the earth vertically at their most northern or southern points from the equator.

Starhawk: Mentioned as an inspiration by many of the contributors to *In the Footsteps of the Goddess,* she is a practicing Wiccan, a peace activist, and the author of one of the first popular books about Goddess worship in the United States, *The Spiral Dance.*

T'ai chi: A series of postures and exercises developed in China as a system of self-defense and as an aid to meditation. T'ai chi is characterized by slow, relaxed, circular movements.

Tara: One of the Indo-European names for the Goddess Earth. In India and Tibet, the Goddess Tara plays an important part in Buddhist Tantric cults in which the female energy is given prominence and has mild and fierce forms which are depicted in five colors: white, green, blue, yellow, and red.

Upper Paleolithic: The last stage of the Old Stone Age (Paleolithic) beginning in approximately 35,000 B.C.E. and lasting for 25,000 and associated with *Homo Sapiens Sapiens*, our direct ancestor.

Wicca or the Craft: In Old English, "wicca" refers to someone who practices witchcraft. It is thought the word derives from the Indo-European roots "wic" or "weik," meaning to bend or turn. Thus a witch who practices "wicca" is able to shape, bend or change reality. Contemporary followers of Wicca are inspired by pre-Christian sources and consider themselves practitioners of ancient European nature religions.

Yoga: An important school of Hindu philosophy with wide influence on all aspects of Hindu thought. The practitioners of yoga practice it to attain higher consciousness and liberation from suffering and ignorance. The physical practice of this philosophy consists of breathing exercises and postures for therapeutic purposes.

Suggested Readings

This is a sampling of the wonderful works in print about the Goddess. Most of the books listed below are available through the KIT Website, www.booktrends.com. So pull up a comfy chair and indulge yourself in this world of inspirational reading.

Ancient Mirrors of Womanhood: A Treasury of Goddess and Heroine Lore from Around the World — Merlin Stone, illustrated by Cynthia Stone (Beacon Press, 1991)

Black Madonnas: Feminism, Religion and Politics in Italy — Lucia Chiavola Birnbaum (Northeastern University Press, 1993)

Celestially Auspicious Occasions: Seasons, Cycles and Celebrations — Donna Henes (Berkley Publishing Group, 1996)

The Chalice and the Blade: Our History, Our Future — Riane Eisler (Harper & Row, 1987)

The Civilization of the Goddess—Marija Gimbutas, edited by Joan Marler (HarperSanFrancisco, 1991)

Crossing the Circle at the Holy Wells of Ireland — Mary and Ted

Brenneman (University Press of Virginia, 1995)

Crossing to Avalon: A Woman's Midlife Pilgrimage — Jean Shinoda Bolen (HarperSanFrancisco, 1994)

Daughters of the Goddess — Linda Johnsen (Yes International, 1994)

Drawing Down the Moon: Witches, Druids, Goddess-Worshippers, and Other Pagans in America Today — Margot Adler (Penguin/Arkana, 1997)

Dreaming the Dark: Magic, Sex and Politics — Starhawk (Beacon Press, 1997)

From the Realm of the Ancestors: An Anthology in Honor of Marija Gimbutas — edited by Joan Marler (Knowledge, Ideas & Trends, Inc. 1997)

The Ghasulian Wall Paintings — Dorothy Cameron (Kenyon-Deane Ltd., 1981)

Goddesses and Gods of Old Europe, 6500-3500 B.C.: Myths, Legends and Cult Images — Marija Gimbutas (University of California Press, 1982)

Grandmother Moon: Lunar Magic in Our Lives: Spells, Rituals, Goddesses, Legends, and Emotions Under the Moon — Zsuzanna Budapest (HarperSanFrancisco, 1991)

The Grandmother of Time: A Woman's Book of Celebrations, Spells, and Sacred Objects for Every Month of the Year — Zsuzanna Budapest (Harper & Row, 1989)

The Great Cosmic Mother: Rediscovering the Religion of the Earth — Monica Sjöö (HarperSanFrancisco, 1991)

Habitations of the Great Goddess — Cristina Biaggi (Knowledge, Ideas & Trends, Inc., 1994)

Holy Book of Women's Mysteries: Feminist Witchcraft, Goddess Rituals, Spellcasting, and Other Womanly Arts — Zsuzanna Budapest (Wingbow Press: Bookpeople, 1989)

Jambalaya: The Natural Woman's Book of Personal Charms and Practical Rituals — Luisah Teish (Harper & Row, 1985)

The Lady of the Beasts — Buffie Johnson (Inner Traditions International, 1994)

The Language of the Goddess — Marija Gimbutas (Harper & Row, 1989)

The Laughter of Aphrodite — Carol Christ (Harper & Row, 1987)

The Living Goddess — Marija Gimbutas, edited and supplemented by Miriam Robbins Dexter (University of California Press, 1999)

Longing for Darkness — China Galland (Viking, 1990)

The Masks of God — Joseph Campbell (Arkana, 1991)
    Creative Mythology
    Occidental Mythology
    Oriental Mythology
    Primitive Mythology

Motherpeace: A Way to the Goddess Through Myth, Art and Tarot — Vicki Noble (Harper & Row, 1983)

Mysteries of the Dark Moon: The Healing Power of the Dark Goddess — Demetra George (HarperSanFrancisco, 1992)

Myths to Live By — Joseph Campbell (Arkana, 1993)

The Once and Future Goddess: A Symbol for Our Times — Elinor W. Gadon (Harper & Row, 1989)

Rebirth of the Goddess: Finding Meaning in Feminist Spirituality — Carol Christ (Routledge, 1997)

The Reflowering of the Goddess — Gloria Orenstein (Pergamon Press, 1990)

Sacred Pleasure: Sex, Myth, and the Politics of the Body — New Paths to Power and Love — Riane Eisler (HarperSanFrancisco, 1995)

Shakti Woman: Feeling Our Fire, Healing Our World: The New Female Shamanism — Vicki Noble (HarperSanFrancisco, 1991)

Songs for Earthlings — edited by Julie Forest Middleton, illustrated by Gwendolyn Rowe, Sylvia Sims, and Heather Alexander (Emerald Earth Publishing, 1998)

The Spiral Dance: A Rebirth of the Ancient Religion of the Great Goddess — Starhawk (HarperSanFrancisco, 1999)

Symbols of Birth and Death in the Neolithic Era — Dorothy Cameron (Kenyon-Deane Ltd., 1981)

Virgin, Mother, Crone: Myths and Mysteries of the Triple Goddess — Donna Wilshire, illustrated by Jim Ann Howard and June Withington (Inner Traditions International, 1994)

When God Was a Woman — Merlin Stone (Harcourt Brace Jovanovich, 1978)

Whence the Goddesses — Miriam Robbins Dexter (Pergamon Press, 1990)

Womanspirit Rising: A Feminist Reader in Religion — edited by Carol Christ and Judith Plaskow (HarperSanFrancisco, 1992)

The text for *In the Footsteps of the Goddess* was set in Bembo. This beautiful and eminently readable typeface was created by Francesco Griffo for Cardinal Bembo's tract "de Aetna" in 1495.

The titles of this book were set in *Medici Script* which was designed by *Herman Zapf for Linotype in 1974*. It is a calligraphic typeface meant to simulate a broad-edged pen on rough paper.